Power of the Secret Place

Bobbie Jean Merck

A Great Love, Inc.
Toccoa, Georgia

Unless otherwise indicated, all scriptural quotations are from the *King James Version* of the Bible.

Power of the Secret Place
ISBN 0-929263-03-0
Copyright © 1990 by
A Great Love, Inc.
P.O. Box 1248
Toccoa, Georgia 30577

Published by
A Great Love, Inc.
P.O. Box 1248
Toccoa, Georgia 30577
U.S.A.

Contents

Introduction

Many books have been written about prayer and its various aspects, and without doubt, they have helped believers develop in their walk with God. This book is not intended to be a "how to" manual, or list of steps to successful prayer. However, the concepts presented, substantiated by scripture, will give the reader a better understanding of the relationship God seeks with His family as they enter into regular communication with Him. In that special relationship, needs are expressed, guidance and direction are given, love is exchanged, and miracles are received.

In my experience, I have found that I must have regular intake of the Word of God. I get hungry to consume scripture and feel somewhat cheated if I don't get to have the Word of God. That does not disallow, disqualify, or discount the work of the Holy Spirit in my life at all. Men were moved upon by the Holy Spirit to speak the Word of the Lord, and write it down. The Holy Spirit will manifest Himself, to us, because He is God. Jesus said, in essence, that the Holy Spirit would speak or manifest what He heard Jesus asking Him to speak or manifest. (See John 16:13,14) He will not disappoint us, nor will He put us to shame.

I believe that God works according to our capacity. He doesn't only work according to our faith, but He works according to our capacity, which is why faith is "ever increasing." Whenever God moves, He prepares the vessel. Many people do not have their desires manifested because they individually are not asking of God, but rather are asking others to seek God on their behalf. When you go to God yourself in prayer, it prepares you to receive from Him.

Almighty God wants us to grow to a place of confidence, trust, and expectation that He will do that which agrees with His Word, if we ask Him. James 4:2 states, "...*ye have not, because ye ask not.*" An application of this verse is apparent when that which is requested is often not received, because the person is depending on someone else to ask God, rather than seeking the Lord for himself. As an outcome of studying about the secret place, it is my desire that each reader enters into the place of knowing Him in greater depth and intimacy. Be blessed in the precious Name of Jesus.

Bobbie Jean

Chapter 1
Jubilee

As a means of laying a foundation for understanding the secret place, I want to share what the Lord gave us for 1989, which has been in effect since Calvary, yet needed to be proclaimed. He instructed me to tell His people, according to Isaiah 61, that it is the Year of Jubilee, and that I was anointed to command, demand, and decree liberty upon His people. He had not called me to pronounce judgment, or predict that you are going through the wilderness and the hard places, but rather, He has provided for our liberty.

According to Leviticus, chapter 25, at the end of every 49 year cycle (seven Sabbath years), there is a Sabbath year designated as the Year of Jubilee. It is a year of redemption, where all the land is returned to its original owner, and slaves are set free.

There is an economic principle involved in that if you buy property near the beginning of the forty-nine year cycle, the value of that property is high, and very expensive. The closer to the forty-ninth year, the less the value of the property became, because during the fiftieth year, the ownership of the property that was purchased reverted back to its original owner, and therefore, did not sell for much.

We are nearing the return of the Lord Jesus Christ, and God said that the closer we get to His return, the less value we are going to put on earthly things. The following prophecy was given during the teaching of this series in Fresno, California, on October 24, 1989, which speaks forth the heart of the Father.

"I Am bringing you to a place, saith God, that you are going to step into things that are unknown to you.

They are most assuredly unknown to you right at this moment in time. Even when I cause you to cross over, saith God, into the realms and into the dimensions of My power, and My might, and My strength, and of My Holy Spirit, and of His glory and grace.

You are not going to comprehend with your natural mind, but you are simply going to go on in that measure of My might and My strength. For it is recorded for My people, that My people are going to be willing in the day of My power (and it is the day of My power upon you, saith God). Do not think that power will be manifest or will come forth without the dimension of love that I have brought into this world system.

For as I gave My Only Son on the cross of glory, the cross of Calvary, the devil would have said, 'It is not a cross of glory.' Man would have said, 'It is not a cross of glory.' But I say it was a cross of glory when My Son was crucified, the Lord of Glory, so that My people could be brought out of darkness; My people could be brought out of deceit. My people could stand upon solid ground on their own two feet. They could come into the Holy of Holies. They could dine with Me. They could visit with Me. They could fellowship and commune with Me, and know it is so sweet, 'I Am a priest unto the most High God. I Am a holy priest, and I Am made holy by the Holy Spirit that *indwells* within Me.'

The power that I have released in your generation shall increase and it shall multiply. It will multiply as the bread out of the very beginning of compassion, and of love — My heart, don't you see.

You will begin to travail. You will begin to groan. You will begin to cry, and you will begin to weep, for you will see mankind. You will see them defeated. You will see them going to hell. You will see them without hope, and you will know, that you know, that you know, that you have within you that ingredient that will cause them to come out of the powers of darkness, out of the throes of hell. They will come and they will be like you. They will stand upon the solid rock, the Christ, the Jesus, on two feet.

They will have the ability, new ability, saith God, that I Am giving unto you. Yes, this very week I Am making deposits that at the moment of time are unknown to you, are ungrasped by you, not understood by you. But as deposits go, saith God, as you continue to follow on to know Me, and to follow Me, yes to trust and obey, you will find deposits of love. You will find deposits of power and might and strength.

For it is the hour, saith God, not only that you begin to pray for one another to be filled with the spirit of boldness, but it is the moment in time when you should begin to pray for one another to know Me and not to be corrupted by flatteries, as one denying the covenant. It is written in My Word, that they know Me, not about Me, not through someone else's testimony, not through someone else's experience, but that you, My people, My born-again believers, My sons and My daughters of God, know Me for yourself. And then it is written, when you know Me, you shall be mighty and you shall do exploits that will explode the natural mind. For there is no limit.

I have set this place as a light in a dark place. I have set this place as a gathering place, saith God: a place where the wounded, a place where the defeated, a place where the wimps can be turned into warriors; a place where you will not ever again be in disgrace, for it is a place that I have ordained that you come into and that you know the fullness of My grace.

For I have provided, saith God, grace for every generation, not unmerited favor, saith God, but I have provided in its own time and in its own season, a grace for every deed; a grace for every failure; a grace for every weakness and every defeat; yea, even grace for rejection; grace for abuse; grace for misuse — Holy Spirit — a grace for misunderstanding, for He is the Holy Spirit of understanding. It shall be much more, saith God, than I have already spoken unto you. It will be grace, My ability, the wonders of My Being, the wonders of My Person. For is it not written, that the place where you come to receive My grace is as you bow upon your knee, as you humble yourself before Me, as you, yourself, enter into the throne room and approach the throne of grace.

As you do not depend upon others to stand in your place before My face, but that you take your position, knowing that you know, I Am the God of all grace. Whatever you can't do, whatever you don't have and whatever you are not, as you come unto Me, I will not turn you away, saith God. For it is also written, as you draw nigh unto Me, I will draw nigh unto you. It is also written, that if you humble yourself before Me, I will exalt you. I will lift you up, I will raise you up.

Yes, just like it has been given testimony, for the time and the season and the place, I will order your steps, and I will direct your paths. But the decision has to be made: *'I'm going to serve God, the Father, the God of all grace. I'm going to be serving the Lord of Grace, and I'm going to do it with the Holy Spirit of grace.'* Seek not to please the face of man or woman, for your faith will not work, as My Son said when He walked in the earth. If you seek to please men, if you seek to please women, it will be one of the final mightiest testings that shall come against thee.

Will you please Me or will you please those about thee? If you will choose, *'It is God whom I trust, and it is God whom I obey,'* you will find that as you come unto Me, I will not only show you the way, I will not only reveal My plan and My will to you, but I will give you My grace, My sufficiency, My efficiency, My power, My strength, My might, My help. I will give you My very own ability.

That's the difference between the old and the new covenants, saith the Spirit of grace. They did not have within them the operation of the living power of grace, the Holy Spirit, Himself. You are born again by the Holy Spirit of grace. So you will see in your generation that you will come to that place in a moment of time, *'I am going to please my God.'* Then, don't you know that everything else will work out just fine. I will move you, and I will take you, and I will direct you. I'll keep you where you ought to be.

It doesn't matter to you, does it, if you know that you know, that it is only My glory that you desire and you long to see? You will find faith working as you have never known faith to work for thee, for I Am calling My people to this day and this hour of My power and My might, to seek Me and to please Me, and to delight themselves in Me, and to be a delight unto Me.

You will find it true in your generation, there is a measure of grace that I Am pouring out upon My people who have an ear to hear what the Spirit is saying, content to be in their place, seeking not the place of another, knowing that I've created them and I've fashioned them, even in their mother's womb I called them. I anointed them, and I appointed them, before the foundations of the world were laid.

For such a time as you stand, saith God, I looked down and I saw you. I knew you had weaknesses, but have I not said that in your weakness, if you will let Me, My strength and My grace will be made strong. So the weaker you are, you are going to be so powerful in My grace, so strong in My grace. For it is those that know they are wimps. It is those who know they are nothing. It is for those who know, *'I can do all things, but I can't do it alone. I must do it with Jesus Christ, who alone doth impart His strength unto me....'*

Oh, I'm looking for people, saith God, that don't depend upon themselves. I'm looking for people, saith God, that don't have emotional dependency upon others. I'm looking to those people that will know that I Am, that I Am, that I Am; and whatever they lack, and whatever need they have, I'm *El Shaddai. I Am more than enough!"*

Five Progressive Themes

We know in part, and we see in part. No one person has it all, and if anyone tells you that they have it all, run from them. We need every part to put the whole together. The Lord only gave me a part and I have to be faithful to give it. I strongly believe in the prophetic command and decree on the Word of God under the Holy Spirit's unction and direction, that when I speak to people, I believe that God Almighty will go to work for those that have an ear to hear what the Spirit is saying. They get excited about it, expect it to happen, and go to the Word of God to see how it will come to pass.

Five progressive themes were given, that is, each one contingent on the appropriation of the one prior, to give us direction on how to walk in the liberty that had been proclaimed. These areas are not new revelations unfounded in scripture, but rather are substantiated in the Word of God to bless each generation.

Worship

In order of progression, the first area is that of worship. Every aspect of worship has a different word and meaning in the original languages of the Bible, for example, in Greek, there are six words for worship. The process of entering the presence of God can be likened unto the tabernacle of the wilderness and the old temple in Jerusalem.

God gave the arrangement of the tabernacle to Moses and it included an entrance gate, a court, the Holy Place, and Holy of Holies, wherein was the presence of God. During the old covenant, only the High Priest had access once a year into the Holy of Holies. Because of the completed work of Jesus, all believers have direct access to the presence of God at all times.

In worship, we enter in through the gates with thanksgiving. *"In everything give thanks: for this is the will of God in Christ Jesus concerning you"* (1 Thessalonians 5:18). We are to continuously walk in thanksgiving toward God for His abundant blessings, great and small. Find yourself in the habit of talking to Him, loving Him so much. Thank Him, thank Him, thank Him. Live a life of thanksgiving.

From there we enter into the courts with praise. I will explain praise as follows because it is the way God gave it to me. Praise is fifty-fifty in terms of its content. Half of your attention is on who He is because it blesses you, and the other half is on the wonderful things He has done for you. In

Hebrew, there are ten words for praise. Some of the nuances of meaning include lifting hands, spinning, jumping, dancing, clapping hands, and speaking the praises of the most High God. After entering the gates with thanksgiving, then into the courts with praise, worship brings us into the Holy of Holies, into the throne room of Almighty God, into the very special intimate secret place.

It is the Holy Spirit of worship Himself that falls upon you, because you have yielded yourself to be thankful and to praise. I love these times when the Holy Spirit just totally envelops me, and I no longer have any thought of myself. There is no thought about what He has done or is going to do on your behalf. The only concern is with the adoration, the love, and the wonderful nature of Almighty God. Frequently there is weeping, not emotional weeping, but the kind that is from the very depths of your being as one is awed by the presence of Almighty God.

One of the many definitions of worship is simply serving Him. Romans 12:1 says to *"...present your bodies a living sacrifice, holy, acceptable unto God."* In several translations including the Phillips, Knox, and Amplified Translation, it states that this is your *"reasonable worship."*

Religion, that is, man's attempt to justify himself before God, has its participants put on little cloaks of praise, worship, and piety when attending a service. True Christianity, however, is a twenty-four hour a day commitment to the Lord. This includes times of worship in church, playing a musical instrument or singing, or just doing your best bellowing like a bullfrog, making a "joyful noise" unto the Lord. It also includes the times doing mundane activities like changing tires, changing diapers, washing, mopping, taking a shower, driving a car, and so on. Worshipping God needs to be a lifestyle for the believer.

Knowing God

The second theme is to know God above all else. This means that no matter what circumstance comes, or what is felt emotionally, or what the situations seem to be, the knowledge that God is greater than every bit of that is the prevailing thought. In those places of testing, *sing to your barrenness* (Isaiah 54:1-2). When prayers are seemingly not producing fruit in your life; when circumstances seem like they are not going to change; when rebellious people look like they are not likely to change, exalt Almighty God in the barrenness of that situation.

Praise and worship Him, telling Jesus that He is Lord. Sing into the barrenness, and see exactly what was declared by the prophet in Isaiah 54:1 and again by Paul in Galatians 4. Exalting Almighty God is one of the keys to overcoming in all of those things. Sing praises to the most High God, love Him, and you will find that the barrenness will become fruitful.

A great example of singing to barrenness is Paul and Silas in that jail at midnight in Acts 16, after they cast the spirit of divination out of the young woman. They were in a dark dungeon cell. It was midnight, cold and damp. The rats and roaches were running across the floor. They were bound and in prison. Things were seemingly not working for them. The scenario might have gone something like this:

"How are you doing, Paul?"

"Well, I'm hangin' in there, Silas. How are you doing?"

"It's awfully cold in here, Paul, and it doesn't smell too good either."

"Let's pray to Him Who is the most High God. Let's praise Elohim. Let's praise Adonai. Let's praise the One Who delivers."

"All right, Paul."

Like anybody who perhaps has not had exquisite training in voice, Paul and Silas began to squeak and croak out their praises at midnight. They praised God for Who He is and expressed love for Him.

Meanwhile, God was sitting on His throne, and all the

angels were around Him. Saints bowed low and worshipped Him, singing the hallelujahs. The heavens were filled with the high praises and worship of Almighty God. It sounded like the voice of multitudes and many, many waters. We cannot comprehend such sound.

God was sitting on His throne and a big angel was standing there, when suddenly God said, "Listen. What is that I hear? I hear somebody praising Me."

"God, all of these people up here are praising and worshipping You and playing their harps. They love You; they adore You. For You they were created, to give You pleasure, praise, worship, and adoration."

God responded, "I know, but I hear another sound and it is coming from down there." And He looked over the banister of heaven to see Paul and Silas praising Him. He liked it so well, that He started tapping His foot. The earth is His footstool, so when he tapped His foot, it caused an earthquake. *The jail shook and the prison bonds fell off.*

Although this is only an imaginary version of what really happened, the issue still remains that praise and worship will do something that nothing else will do. It will set the captive free. It will cause you to give birth where you have been barren. It will cause prayers to be answered. That is why David said in Psalm 34:1, *"I will bless the Lord at all times: His praise shall continually be in my mouth."*

Praise is the highest form of faith, because when our mouth is filled with praise, we cannot speak doubt and unbelief, or murmuring and complaining. The more we praise and worship God, the more we develop. The more we desire to praise, the more we need to praise. We increase and enlarge our capacity. We come to know God above all else when we worship Him. Our trust and confidence is going to be in Him.

When we come to the place of knowing Him, we are able to say, "I know how to be abased. I know how to abound. It matters not. The only thing that matters to me is that I am in the perfect will of Almighty God, that I am delighting Him, and that I am pleasing Him."

All cares will be cast over on Him. We know that He is greater than it all, and that He loves us so much that He will never disappoint us.

Rest

God said that after we know Him above all else, there would be rest. He gave me Hebrews, chapters 3 and 4, about entering into His rest. He said that two things keep people from entering into His rest. One is disobedience, which comes from a hard heart, and the other is not combining the Word with faith.

Rest, like faith, is for now. The Lord said to me, *"Quit waiting for Me to do something. I am doing it today. Tomorrow will never come."* If we wake up every day thinking God is going to do something tomorrow, next month, next year, it will never happen, because tomorrow never comes.

This rest will come after worship, and after knowing God above all else. *Rest means we cease from our own flesh works.* We do everything we know to do. We pray, building ourselves up on our most holy faith; praying in our natural language; praying in tongues; worship God; study the Word; meditate on the Word; prepare; but then having done all to stand, we stand. We rest in the Holy Spirit. We let the Holy Spirit work.

We enter into rest because we know as we have never known before, God is in control. He is bigger than everything, including sickness, financial indebtedness, or rebellion. God is greater than it all.

Building the Kingdom of God

After worship, knowing God, and rest, the fourth theme has to do with the hearts of God's people wanting to build the church of the Lord Jesus Christ; to build the kingdom of God; *to seek and save that which is lost.* The Lord gave me Matthew 6:33 and the entire book of Haggai.

The church has recently gone through a period of time learning its identity and position in Christ. We have also heard much on how to get our finances to bless us. We should have learned to put our priorities and motives in the right biblical perspective. *Our goal for obtaining wealth should be to take the gospel of the Lord Jesus Christ to the ends of the earth, and to build the local church.* God's people should be motivated by His love and purposes. That is why we believe Him for increases and promotions.

Central to the kingdom of God is the Great Commission, getting people out of the pits of hell into the kingdom of God. There is an anointing for souls on the church, whether apostles, prophets, evangelists, pastors, teachers, ministers of helps. *We are all ministers of reconciliation.* We are all witnesses of Jesus. We are all ministers of the glorious gospel of Jesus Christ. Our prayers, our ministry, our growing, our making money, our whole living should have as its purpose, plan, and goal, to see men, women, and children brought out of hell into the kingdom of God, and to see the church be built up.

In the local church, there will be a knitting together unlike anything ever seen before. Those ordained by God to be together, are going to be knit together by the bond of perfection, which is a love that will fight for each other instead of hypocrisy. One of the words for friends in the Bible is the same word in Psalm 23:1, *"The Lord is my shepherd."* It literally means *"feeder."* The friends you have should feed you.

In Georgia some plants have a peculiar branch growing from them. This peculiar branch is called a sucker. That sucker has one aim, that is to draw forth the nourishment and strength from the main part of the plant so that the plant will not produce fruit on the other branches. Your friends should not be like those suckers, drawing out of you the very vitality and nourishment of Almighty God that keeps you from producing everlasting fruit to the glory of God.

Your friends should be feeders, and you should be a

feeder to them. If the body is functioning properly, the exchange is such, that all benefit, grow, and produce fruit.

In the book of Haggai, there is a powerful indictment that has implications for the church even though it is in the Old Testament. As Paul said, *"All scripture is given by inspiration of God, and is profitable for doctrine, for reproof, for correction, for instruction in righteousness"* (2 Timothy 3:16). Also, in 1 Corinthians, chapter 10, we are admonished that the Word was given to be an example for us.

As in Haggai, sometimes God's people have built large edifices, and have not done one thing for God. Then He says, "Don't cry out because your crops aren't producing. Don't cry out because it's not working. Plagues and blights and destructions have come against you." Haggai tells us to do just one thing, *make an adjustment.* Change your attitude, motive, plan, and purpose. If you will do it, the glory of the latter house shall be greater than that of the former. *Repentance only brings greater glory, never shame.*

Matthew 6:33 works together with the same idea, *"But seek ye first the kingdom of God, and his righteousness; and all these things shall be added unto you." In doing this* you cannot keep the blessings of God from overtaking you.

Be of An Upright Mind

For the fifth theme, the Lord said that the future is for those of an upright mind. He specifically gave me Psalm 25:4, which says, *"Shew me thy ways, O Lord; teach me thy paths."* In Hebrew, it literally means, "Show me Your next course of events. Don't let me be left out of anything."

When we don't change and move on with God, we cease worshipping Him. We stop reverencing and fearing Him. Religion sets in along with all of its baggage. Psalm 55:19 declares, *"...Because they have no changes, therefore they fear not God."* Change in us must happen in order for us to go from faith to faith, and from glory to glory.

New Agers don't hold the future in their hands.

Neither do the occult, Satan worship, world religions, or even Wall Street or governments. It is for those who will trust and obey. It is for those who are of an upright mind. *"And be renewed in the spirit of your mind"* (Ephesians 4:23). The word "spirit" means to have the same attitude, aim, and purpose as that of the Lord Jesus Christ.

Rise up in the morning saying, "What is it today, Father?" Or just love Him and do what you are supposed to do. Let God be God in your life. Enter into rest knowing He will order your steps, direct your paths, and He will never be late. He will have you in the right place, at the right time. Not only will you be there, but you will have the equipment. You will have the perfection that you need up to that moment of time.

We can be what God created us to be. We just need God the Father, the Son, and the Holy Spirit. Get out of that rut of trying to please everybody else but God. Not everybody is called to the same tribe, metaphorically speaking.

Jacob had twelve sons who became the patriarchs of the tribes of Israel. One was a tribe of wisdom. Issachar understood the times so that they could provide understanding to their nation (1 Chronicles 12:32).

Not everyone is a praiser like the tribe of Judah. Let those that are of the tribe of Judah shout, dance, clap. Let them do it all. Not everybody is like the tribe of Benjamin, the mighty warring tribe of Israel. Some people are just not going to war. It's not that they lack fortitude, it's just that they don't belong to the warring tribe. It's all wrapped up in Jesus, but let each person in the body of Christ be what God decided that he should be before the foundations of the world were laid. (See Genesis 49:8,27)

There is not a human being alive that is going to amount to a hill of beans without the grace of God and without His gifts and callings in operation. We must love as God loves. We certainly do not want to encourage error or excess, but we must stop childish backbiting and take disagreements to the prayer closet. God can change people and put strength into their weaknesses as well as our own. We have all called out for mercy in the time of weakness. James 2:13 says, "*...mercy rejoiceth against judgment.*"

Romans 12:21 tells us that when someone does evil against us, we overcome that evil with good. Heap coals of fire on their head, as is stated in Romans 12:20. This does not mean to burn them up, or burn evil out of them, or any other such judgment. It simply means that when someone is acting in an evil manner, their fire has gone out and all they have left is a few dying embers. Our response is to take the white-heated love coals of fire, the love and zeal of Jesus, and pour it upon them. Heap the coals of love and mercy.

It is putting into practice the two great commandments given by Jesus that sum up all the others, to love God with your whole being, and your neighbor as yourself, which is the natural outgrowth of loving God. These five themes — worship, knowing God, rest, building the kingdom of God, and being of an upright mind — are necessary if we are to walk in Jubilee. Yet, the revelation of this for your life comes in the secret place.

Dwelling in the Secret Place

Psalm 91 declares, "*He that dwelleth in the secret place of the most High shall abide under the shadow of the Almighty.*" The understanding of the secret place is something that will probably increase, solidify, or openly strengthen that which you may already be doing, and yet point you in a direction of change, sensitivity, and alertness for your own life.

To begin with, it is not what is done behind the pulpit, in front of it, in the work place, or in the home that determines your God, but rather what is done in the secret place. Everything is not always as it seems on the surface. *What we do in our secret place reveals who and what our god is.*

If I just seek time to relax or indulge in some preoccupation, then that becomes my god. If I seek time to be with the

Almighty God, to worship Him, and have fellowship with Him, then He is my God.

What we do, think, act, read, watch, listen to, or speak, when nobody else is looking, reveals how we relate or don't relate to God. What we do in public is less important than what we do alone, because there is no one to monitor our behavior. It is a place of honesty because no one is there to judge us or determine our spiritual condition.

Psalm 91 clearly gives the conditional statement that if we dwell in the secret place of the most High, it is then that we shall abide under His shadow. God has emphasized the importance of the secret place. It is because what is done in secret is a reflection of our aims and purposes regarding the kingdom of Jesus Christ.

Paul says in the epistle to the Romans, that you become a slave to that which you serve. How free can we be from bondage? We can be as free as we want to be. If we live our lives as an open book, honest, upright, and without fear of man's disapproval, Satan cannot put us into bondage again. God desires us to be open books and prepares us for a life of liberty in the secret place.

Secret things have power that we have not understood before, but we are beginning to see that it is the secret place that determines what ultimately comes forth in public. That which is hidden is brought to light.

In God's Word, there are things that He wants done in private. It seems that the things God wants done in private, the world system wants to bring out into the public. That is most apparent in mass media. This lack of order has slipped into the church.

God intended groaning and travail in intercession to be done in the secret place, and immature intercessors want to bring it out in public. When this has been done, it has caused division, problems, and confusion. This has never been the case when one person is doing it alone in the prayer closet as unto the Lord.

We Are Not Are Own

It is in the secret place in the prayer closet where God is established in every area of our lives. In many of the countries I travel to for ministry, I am always impressed with how believers live for Christ. They don't live for themselves. They know that nothing belongs to them. They understand that they are simply stewards of whatever God has entrusted to them, whether it be the anointing, ministry gifts, finances, or anything else.

We need to understand that we are not our own; we are bought with a price, the blood of Jesus Christ. We must glorify God, and we are going to know that everything that we have, everything we are, spirit, soul, body, materially, whatever, belongs to Almighty God. We must become committed to getting His work done, and to please God at all cost.

The body of Christ is moving together in this direction. When God unites spirit to spirit, deep calling to deep, iron sharpening iron, He is putting us together, not to be fascinated with each other, or to be impressed by each other, or to boast in our belonging to a particular group, but rather to fulfill the plan of God in a particular area. He has called each of us to be a link in the chain.

You Are His Workmanship

The body of Christ is tired of pretense, pretending one thing and being another. The secret places reveal what you really are. God loves you just the way you are, not what others want to make of you. God says we are transformed into His image, from glory to glory, by the Holy Spirit and the Word of God. We are not to transform each other into the image that we have for each other. The Lord has an image of you that He alone wants. He does not have carbon copies, just as there is only one Jesus. None of us even has a complete image of ourselves. God has the pattern that He has laid for each of us, and it is wonderful.

As His workmanship, you are fearfully and wonderfully made. Before the foundations of the world were laid, He said,

16

"There she is; there he is. In the end of the end days, they are the ones I can trust. They are the ones that I can mold. They are the ones that I can shape and transform. I know they will do what I have for them to do."

As we come into the unity in the faith and in the knowledge of the Son of God, the Lord Jesus Christ, maturing into Him, *"we are no longer tossed about by every wind of doctrine"* (Ephesians 4:14). The body of Christ needs to recognize unity in the faith in the knowledge of the Lord Jesus Christ. We need to make every effort to keep the unity of the Spirit through the bond of peace. Then the unity of the glory will be ours. He will manifest Himself, and this is what is really important.

For that to happen, God is moving us into the right place, cutting right into the heart of the matter because He knows what we think down deep inside. He knows what we do when nobody else is looking. He knows what is shaping and transforming us. God is saying, "I want you free." *It is the Year of Jubilee, the year of liberty and redemption.* Everything that is done in secret, should be done as if it were an open book.

"He that dwelleth in the secret place of the most High shall abide under the shadow of the Almighty" (Psalm 91:1), means that if in your spare time, your secret time and place, your primary motivation, aim, attitude, and purpose is Almighty God, then you will dwell under His shadow.

Conversely, you will not dwell under His shadow if other things, and other people, are your secret place. When we work His works, as the psalmist declared, this is what we will say of the Lord, *"He is my refuge; He is my fortress; My God in Him I will trust. Surely, He shall deliver me from the snare of the fowler and from the noisome pestilence. He shall cover me with His feathers, and under His wings I shall trust. His truth is my shield and my buckler."* The truth does not work until we make God our foremost companion in the secret place.

Chapter 2
Effects of the Secret Place

While ministering on the secret place in Fresno, California, the Holy Spirit gave the following prophecy on October 24, 1989. It is significant to what the Lord is doing in His universal church.

"For I Am bringing you into My very bosom. I Am bringing you unto Myself, for I Am drawing you unto Myself by My Spirit. I Am bringing you to that place that John entered into and that John knew as My Son walked upon the earth, for it is a private decision. It is a personal decision. Will you know Me, or will you know about Me?

And, as My Son asked the question, 'Who do you say that I Am?' I Am not interested in what others say for you to hear, and for you to repeat what they say that I Am, but I ask you, as My child; I ask you as My earthen vessel; I ask you, Who do you say that I Am? For it is the time and it is the day, and it is the hour that if you would prevail against the gates of hell, if they would not slow you up, you must have your own personal revelation of Who I Am, saith Jesus, the Christ. You must know for yourself that I Am your Messiah, I Am your anointed One. I Am the One that sets the captives free. I Am the One that heals the broken-hearted. I Am the One that binds up the wounded. I Am the One that causes the recovery of sight to be manifested unto you.

For there is much spiritual blindness. There have been those who have chosen to believe the doctrines and the traditions of men, and, therefore, because they have doubted, and they have not believed Me, the god of this world has

19

been able to blind the eyes of those who believe not Me. You see, Hebrew is not the final authority, and neither is Greek the final authority according to and upon My Word, saith God Almighty. But, I the Holy Spirit, speak unto thee, and I say that I Am the final authority upon the Word of God, for it is I Who gave the Word of God. It was men moved and borne along on the wind of the Holy Spirit, Myself, inspired of Me, that brought the revelation, illumination, the great truths that are now what you call the Bible, the Word of God, don't you see. So, if you would prevail in the hour that is come, know the Holy Spirit.

It is an hour of power, it is an hour of might. It is also an hour of truth, for there can be no ultimate power, and there can be no ultimate might without there being truth. My Word is truth, but it is not the interpretation of man, but it is the interpretation of the Holy Spirit. There may be many applications of truth of My Word, but there is only one interpretation, and it is given by the voice of the Holy Spirit.

It is the day and the hour when you are to come to know the Holy Spirit. You are to come to recognize His movings and His leadings, for He does come suddenly, and He goes just as suddenly. He comes with the wind, and He comes as the wind. He comes here, and He goes there. He blows here, and He blows there. You do not know where He is coming from, and you do not know where He is going, but I have given you instruction to go with the wind. I say that it is sudden, because one moment it is not, and the next moment it is. Yes, He does come softly. He does come softly.

I Am training My people as a mighty, mighty, mighty, mighty, mighty group of people. I Am training them. I Am training them. They must hear the Master's voice, and they must know the Master's voice. Therefore, they must know the leading and the guiding and the moving of the Holy Spirit. He will point you in the right direction.

I Am drawing you unto Myself. I Am drawing unto My bosom those that have a desire, that have a heart to come close to Me. I draw nigh unto those who draw nigh unto Me. John was called the apostle of love, and he was the one of whom My Son said was the beloved. Yes, he could not be killed, though he was tortured beyond natural endurance of natural man. He could not be taken by natural man because he was that apostle of love. He had the deposit of love. He had the transference of love. He had the anointing of love. Because he drew nigh unto My Son (it was His decision, you see), as he drew nigh unto My Son, he knew the very heart-beat of My Son, and therefore, he did not walk to the beat of a different drummer. He walked with Me, and he talked with Me, saith God, the Almighty, the Father God.

It is that hour and that time when I Am drawing you unto Myself. Yes, it is that hour, and it is that time, because I long to use you, and I long to bless you, and I long to man-ifest back unto you everything that I have spoken unto you. I long to fulfill every promise that has been made real and alive unto you. I Am not the God that withholds. I Am the God that gives. That which I give is good, and it is perfect.

I do not change, but I do move on. And I Am moving on in your day. I have tried to train you to keep up with the legs of a man, but now you are learning to keep up with the legs of a horse, for I Am giving you the spirit and the anoint-ing of Elijah, where you can outrun any opposing chariot. You can know, that you know, that you know, that now it is the time to run with the vision. The vision will be made clearer, and clearer, and clearer, and you will be more accu-rate in your interpretation of the vision.

Therefore, you will be more successful in your opera-tion and in your output of the vision. Scales are being removed from My people's eyes, saith God, for I Am caus-ing the blind to see. And I Am opening up revelations. I Am opening mysteries. I Am opening up secrets. The light is getting brighter and brighter. It is exposing more and more of My truth. That is why these are the days of light upon you.

They are not as it seems, and they are not as it is in the world, the days of darkness and the days of evil. It is the day of My mercy upon you. It is the day of My goodness upon you. It is the day of My glory upon you. It is the day of light upon you.

Do not be deceived, the angel of light shall not be able to counterfeit the light that is the Light, My Son, Jesus, the Christ. For the light of Him will make that which is of the world, and that which is of the angel of light, appear as darkness. It shall increase upon the earth, and you shall know that it is dense darkness, but it shall not come nigh unto those who will arise and shine and know that their light, the Light of the world, Jesus, the Christ, has arisen upon them. It, the darkness of this world, shall not even touch them.

They shall stand, and they will look to the left, and they will see a thousand fall at their left side; and they will look to the right, and they shall see ten thousand fall at their right side. And oh, it shall be that plague and disease shall try to come upon many of My people, but they will simply stand their ground upon the solid rock, Who is Jesus, the Christ, and none other shall they stand upon.

They will look to the left, and they will see a thousand who refuse to bow their knee and call upon My Name, fall at their left side. And, they will look to the right, and they will see ten thousand fall because they refuse to bow their knee, but it shall not come nigh unto them. They will go forward; they will go free.

'Security' is the watchword of this hour for My people, saith God, confidence and security and trust in the living God. Is there any other God? I know none. I know no other God. I, and I alone, Am God. And if you serve Me, you will not be defeated; you will be successful. If you come along with Me, you will never be brought to shame; you will never be put to shame. For it is written in My Word, which shall never fail you, for I Am bound by My Word, it is written that if you will call upon His Name, the Name that is above all names, you will never be put to shame. You will never be ashamed. For you will shine. You will shine as lights in darkness. You will hold forth the word of life to those that are reaching out.

I will give you many. Do not say that it is coming. Do

not say that just a little longer and the harvest will be ripe for reaping. Do not say that we have to get this building in order. Do not say that we have to get this bank account in order. Do not say that I have to wait for this or that, but go forth into the fields of harvest, saith God, and reap the harvest that is yours.

This is the way you are going to multiply in this day and in this hour. It is the power upon the body, and the body will be a witness wherever they are. The true body, the bride of the Lord Jesus Christ, shall shine as the bride, and they shall be a witness in their place of employment, and they shall be a witness wherever they go.

And, yes, you thought the anointing upon Charles Finney was something to read about and shout about. For when he would walk into a place, it would cause the whole place to shut down at the awesome presence of His presence, the presence of Jesus, the presence of the Holy Spirit upon the man, Charles Finney. But I say unto you, I Am distributing, and I Am putting upon the people in the body, that same kind of glory in this day and in this hour, for it must be strong, saith God. It must shine, saith God. Therefore, it will be upon you, and people will look at you, and they will think, *'There's something strange about that individual; there's something peculiar about that individual.'*

It will be like My Son, even when they tried to throw Him off the cliff, He was so in My anointing, and so in My glory, that He just passed through the midst of them. And so shall it be: no harm shall befall thee if you will obey Me. You can go wherever I direct you to go; you can go wherever I tell you to go. If you will just obey Me, you will be protected, and no harm shall befall thee.

You will see, at thy very own appearance, many shall fall, and they shall say unto thee: *'Show me that which has been given unto thee, for there is something about thee that is different, and I want to know exactly what it is. Would you please deposit that upon me?'* Like Simon, the sorcerer, they will come, and they will say, *'I want to buy this. I want you to give this to me.'* For you see, there is such an anointing being deposited upon My people that it makes the angel of light's anointing look like darkness.

Yes, it is the hour of Jannes and Jambres again, saith God. But as in the day of Moses, you will know that they have reached their end, and they have reached their limit. It may look like they're winning. It may look like they're gaining, saith God, but know there are more of you than of them.

Do not be discouraged, and just know; just know that you, you, and you, and you, and every one of you, I will use for My purpose. I will use for My plan. I will use for My glory. If you will only come unto Me and learn of Me, I will use you for others to see, and to rise up in great victory and glee, because the enemy has had to flee.

I will rend the heavens, saith God. I will let My glory shine through and shine down upon those who have been willing to pay the price, upon those who have come to understand just a little bit, for you can never in that life understand the totality and the fullness of My Son's sacrifice. But those who love their lives not unto death, shall overcome by the blood of the Lamb, and shall overcome by the Word of their testimony, and you shall see Jesus, the Christ, the anointed One move in your midst.

For the Holy Spirit is going to be so much more than just tongues. He is going to be so much more than just righteousness, peace, and joy. He is going to be so much more than just an experience. The day is at hand, saith God, when it will be as it is recorded in My Word, '*It seemeth good to the Holy Ghost and to us.*' And it will be that My people will come to know Him, they will listen to Him, and their visions, their operations, their administrations, and their manifestations shall be orchestrated by the Holy Spirit. For it is His hour, saith God."

As is clearly indicated, God is yearning for a people who will seek Him, forsaking all else. The intensity of this revelation, and the promises of Psalm 91, will be found and determined in the secret place, when nobody else is looking and where no one but God has access.

Be An Open Book

In 1 Samuel 16:7, God told Samuel that He did not look on the outward appearance, but He judged what was in the heart. He let us know that we are prone to make assessments on that which is public, but God looks down into the very innermost parts of our being.

We know from experience that when negative things are revealed, it is an embarrassment, and a hindrance. One of the main keys to living free is to live our lives as an open book. Not that we are not entitled to privacy, but if our private lives are above reproach, we walk in liberty. We do not have to hide from anybody. There is no shame, because we have confidence that we are living our lives to please Almighty God. It is that we are His delight and His pleasure.

Why does God look upon the heart? Why does He look when nobody else is looking? It is because in that place the God, or god, we serve is determined. What is planted as seed in the darkness of the earth, eventually takes root and breaks forth to the surface in the light. So it is with the hidden places of each person.

Secrets have a lot of power. Things that are done in secret, whether good or evil, have more power than when they are done in public. Life is governed by what is done in secret, not by what is done or declared in public. However, the desire to be alone needs to be balanced.

Isolation and seclusion can be dangerous if it is disproportionate with the rest of your life and walk with God. Nevertheless, every person needs to follow the example of the Lord Jesus Christ and find time to be alone with Almighty God in harmony with all other aspects of the Christ life. We cannot pray, or worship Almighty God in the presence of a single human being, like we can when we are all alone with Him.

Psalm 91 says, "...*in the secret place of the most High.*" That is where the promises of that Psalm, as well as the rest of the Word of God, begin to take place and are released to us. It is when we pursue God in the secret place, that we abide in the shadow of the most High.

The condition of abiding in the shadow of the most High has a lot of meanings. One of them is abiding totally under the protection and power of the Holy Spirit. Like Mary in Luke 1:35, the Holy Spirit, Himself, shall come upon thee.

When He talks about the shadow of the Almighty God, He is talking about the Holy Spirit. That is why in Acts 5:15, you find that at the shadow of Peter, people were healed and miracles happened. It wasn't Peter's shadow, but it was the shadow of the Holy Spirit, Himself.

Nothing that I do in public puts me in the shadow of the most High. It is not ministering behind the pulpit, or doing all of the things that we do in the Name of the Lord Jesus Christ in public that puts us in the shadow of His wing, but it is what we do privately. It is what we do when we are alone with Him.

The life that we live secretly determines whose shadow is over us. What I do privately determines the shadow that is over me, whether it is the shadow of God, or whether it is the shadow of flesh, or whether it is the shadow of the adversary.

Preparing For Greatness

God has plans right now beyond anything that our minds can conceive. We can't even imagine what God has in store for us. The secret place should be a message of encouragement, because God never goes to the root unless He is preparing us for greatness.

A friend of mine, Jeanne Wilkerson, who has gone on to be with the Lord, once told me that the longer it takes for a prophecy to be fulfilled in a person's life, over a church, or over a ministry, the greater the work of Almighty God and the greater the vision. In other words, it is the greatness of the thing that God has prophesied that takes longer to fulfill. I would not argue dogmatically over it, but I have experientially found it to be true, and see some scriptural evidence.

We could look at the birth of Jesus. It took four thousand years for the Incarnation, even though we know that God planned it before the foundations of the world were laid. Nevertheless, it shows us the length of time it takes sometimes for prophecy to be fulfilled.

We trust that if it concerns us personally, it would not take four thousand years, and that it would be fulfilled in our lifetime. We should not be discouraged when the prophecies are not fulfilled instantly or in a short span of time. There is a greater dimension to those prophecies.

To illustrate this, a church in Africa had received a prophecy many years ago. Years and years passed, and the Word of the Lord that the glory of God was going to move into that church had not yet been fulfilled. Some of the faithful people of the church received that Word of the Lord and were diligently waiting.

Some people became discouraged and stopped expecting anything to happen. They would pray, and again become enthused. They felt that it would be the church in which the glory was to be manifested. Then again they left because the prophecy was seemingly not fulfilled. The glory of God did not move in when they thought it should. However, there was a group who held on with the pastor.

Thirty-three years from the date of the prophecy, on a Sunday morning, they really had not even been thinking about the prophecy. That Sunday morning, the pastor stood to minister, but God decided He would be the only minister. The glory of God started at the back of the church, and just moved in over the congregation.

The sad part about it was that some people had not prepared their hearts for the glory of God. They had secret lives having the wrong shadow over them. They had secret lives that nobody knew about, except for the devil, their own flesh, and most importantly, God knew about it. Because they were not living as they should in the secret places, when the glory moved in, they were rolling on the floor as the demons came in contact with the glory of God. When the glory moves in, flesh and demons move out. There is only room for the glory. In 1 Kings 8, when the glory moved in, those priests could not stand to minister.

Crossroads to Revival

God is getting us ready. He is going down to the very root, because He wants the glory to move in, and He wants us to experience it for our generation. We are at a point of breakthrough, a crossroad. What do we do with break-throughs? What do we do with crossroads? Does the thought of the glory just tickle our appetite, or do we want it like Jesus, when He was on the Mount of Transfiguration?

His disciples wanted to build three tabernacles there. They did not want to go down. However, for the glory of God to move in, and the Holy Spirit to work, there is one pur-pose only and that is to go down off the Mount of Transfigu-ration and minister to the people who have needs. That is the whole purpose of revival.

Revival is not for the world. Revival is for the saints of God, because you cannot revive something that has not been alive. Revival is for the church of the Lord Jesus Christ, to make it so hot that it is consumed with the all consuming fire of Almighty God. The first indication of revival is that back-sliders begin to slide back to Jesus. Those that have left will come back full of the fire, repentance, love, and power of Almighty God.

Another indicator is the believers, wherever they are, at the supermarket, gas station, or burger-place, are going to minister Jesus on a one-to-one basis. They are going to be doing the signs that follow the believer. They are going to be leading people to the Lord Jesus Christ. They are going to be believing God for the manifestations of the gifts of the Holy Spirit through their lives. Gifts of the Holy Spirit such as a word of knowledge, and bowl the world system off its feet. This is the way revival begins to happen.

It is not only by filling a stadium with one hundred thousand people. It is going to be when God's people get on fire for Jesus. People always come to see a fire.

What Will You Say?

What will you say when you have made that decision to let God have your secret place? As the psalmist did in Psalm 91:2, you will say, "...*the Lord, He is my refuge and He is my fortress: my God, in Him will I trust.*" That is how you can know when God is your secret place.

You trust Him; you know He is your refuge; you know He is your fortress. You are going to say, "*Surely, He shall deliver me from the snare of the fowler, and from the noisome pestilence. He shall cover me with His feathers, and under His wings I shall trust. His truth shall be my shield and my buckler,*" and all the rest of what Psalm 91 declares.

Truth comes forth, when God is our secret place. We will not have to worry about error or deception. We will not have to be concerned about a spirit of wisdom, revelation, knowledge, or understanding. When Almighty God is our secret place, truth will come forth. It is one of the fruits of the secret place.

People operate in the ministry day in and day out as a royal priest. Simply stated, it means ministering to people. They are not a holy priest first to Almighty God, having time with Him, worshipping Him and having Him as their secret place. They give until they lose every bit of strength. They lose their life source, and then begin to operate in the flesh.

The next step is with the enemy, because they have got to keep things going. They have to keep up a facade. That is when exposure comes. That which is hidden is then revealed, and you find things that hurt and disappoint the body of Christ. It is because God is not their secret place. It is because they are not first a holy priest to Almighty God before they are a royal priest unto mankind.

We can pray for one another, bind the enemy, pray to be strong, but understand that foremost, we need to be a holy priest to God. We do not need to be taking each other's time continuously, when God is available.

We should allow the pastor and others to take time alone with God. Wives need to allow husbands time to be alone with Almighty God and not feel threatened. Husbands need to allow wives time to be alone with God and not feel jealous. Even though our relationship is valuable and precious, nobody can take the place of Almighty God in our lives, Whose we are and Whom we serve.

We can be born again and baptized in the Holy Spirit and still have another god before us in the secret place, that is, things that crowd out God. All of Psalm 91 is the secret place for which we are searching. It is the secret time that we spend with the Lord. We appear so spiritual before people, but God looks at what is done in the secret place, and what is done on the inside — aims, motives, attitudes, and purposes. This can only be known by us individually, and by God.

"And be renewed in the spirit of your mind" (Ephesians 4:23). That word *"spirit"* in Greek refers to aim, attitude, motive, and purpose. In Revelation 19:10, the same word is used there about the spirit of prophecy. It has to be the aim, attitude, purpose and motive of the Lord Jesus Christ. Regardless whether you have known the Lord or even been in ministry fifty years or fifty days, motives need to be pure, holy, and in agreement with Almighty God, and need to be checked continuously.

Rewards of the Secret Place

Great is the reward of the secret place, be it good or evil. Matthew 6:1 says, *"Take heed that you do not your alms before men, to be seen of them: otherwise ye have no reward of your Father which is in heaven."* It is interesting to note that in Greek, the word "alms" means righteousness.

In other words, we are not to do righteousness before men to be approved of them, because we will have had our reward already. Righteous deeds include alms giving, but they also include praise, worship, prayer, intercession, and others.

The next verse in Matthew chapter 6 says, *"Therefore when thou doest thine alms, do not sound a trumpet before thee, as the hypocrites do in the synagogues and streets, that they may have glory of men. Verily, I say unto you, They have their reward."* God is our Father, no matter what. When we are born again, regardless of the secret place, He is our Father. If we choose the reward of men, seeing and knowing what we do, that means we do not have a reward from our Father, Almighty God.

These two verses are specifically speaking of giving. What is our motive for giving? Not just finances, but what is our motive for giving anything — a message in tongues, an interpretation, a prophecy, a praise, a dance before the Lord? Even in our complimenting of people, what is the motive? If your motive is pure, you will know and appoint it back up to the Father, Son, and Holy Spirit because you understand, *"I am what I am by the grace of God."*

God does not require us to become experts on knowing how to release the realm of the spirit. He requires us to become as children in faith, simple and pure. In other words, we do not manipulate the Spirit of God and make Him work. We must cooperate with the Holy Spirit.

When people feign the move of God, people get hurt in the name and move of the Holy Spirit. God has times and seasons. It may not be time for things to happen the way that we think they ought to happen.

God is powerful and glory is power. God knows what He is doing. He has that glory for us, the move of the Spirit, but some have tried to make it happen. Havoc and hurt have been the result rather than the exalting of God. We do not need to be as hypocrites.

Many years ago I heard a wonderful pastor teach as a warning, that some people's sins are found out soon, but others are not found out until a much later time. Be that as it may, the sin is going to be exposed. It may be now or it may be later, but it is coming. Everything that is done in secret is going to be revealed in the light.

He also warned about judging other people when their sins are revealed. He gave an illustration of a couple in his church who came down hard on another couple who got a divorce. In time, that very couple's son and daughter-in-law were divorced. That pastor warned that whatever we judge, whatever we criticize about other people's lives, we are sowing seed, not only for ourselves, but for our posterity.

We are fruit inspectors, but we are not to judge another human being. That is God's prerogative and privilege. If we are serious about the kingdom, we must leave these things with God. It would spare us a lot of trouble. To be sure, the secret place has its rewards, both good and evil.

Matthew 6:6 says, *"But thou, when thou prayest, enter into thy closet, and when thou hast shut thy door, pray to thy Father which is in secret...."* Where is your Father? He is in secret. It would seem to me that the best place to praise and worship, pray, do everything else, is in secret.

Of course, good works can be done in public. The Lord receives it, but He also looks in secret. It is what is done in secret places that gives God, the devil, or flesh such power and consequences over our lives.

The Enemy's Secret Place

He sitteth in the lurking places of the villages: in the secret places doth he murder the innocent: his eyes are privily set against the poor.

He lieth in wait secretly as a lion in his den: he lieth in wait to catch the poor: he doth catch the poor, when he draweth him into his net.

He croucheth, and humbleth himself, that the poor may fall by his strong ones.

Psalm 10:8-10

It is in the secret places where people are caught, trapped and killed by the enemy. How does the devil overcome the innocent one? He must first draw him into the wrong secret place. Everyone, without exception knows what it means to be tempted, to be drawn into the secret place by the devil.

The devil's ultimate goal is to do exactly what is said in Psalm 10:8, *"to murder the innocent."* It is the innocent that he wants in those places. Follow the wisdom of Proverbs. We must learn to let God order our steps. When the first step seems like we are going into a secret place where the enemy could kill or steal, we must turn that foot and go in another direction. We must learn that when a contrary thought to the obedience of Jesus Christ for our lives comes in our mind, we immediately must say, *"I resist that thought in the name of the Lord Jesus Christ. It doesn't belong to me. It is contrary to the obedience of the Lord Jesus Christ for my life."*

Hebrews 9:14 says that my conscience is purged from every dead, evil work by the power of the blood of the Lord Jesus Christ. Release the blood of the Lord Jesus Christ over your minds, and immediately begin to say, *"Bless the Lord, O my soul: and all that is within me, bless His holy name!"* Get that wrong thought out immediately. Your foot never takes a step that your mind has not first ordained it to take.

We may be all peace and joy in public, but how are things in private? How are things in the secret place? We are not going to let the enemy do that to us. We are not going to let him draw us into his secret place.

He is against the poor. He *"lieth in wait to catch the poor."* The enemy is the one that forces, pushes and shoves. The Holy Spirit guides and leads. The Holy Spirit is gentle.

I asked the Lord one time, why the cult representatives are so sweet, and do things for people, whereas others who name the Name of Jesus are sometimes everything but sweet. What is going on? We ought to be the sweetest.

He answered me saying, *"I'll tell you what it is. It's seduc-*

ing spirits. They are so sweet, like honey drawing a fly into its trap. Once they get those people into that trap, it's too late." The enemy draws like a magnet.

There is a verse of scripture that says, *"I will set no wicked thing before mine eyes..."*(Psalm 101:3). If you observe lying vanities, you forsake your own mercy (Jonah 2:8). We cannot follow these things. We must keep a guard on our sense gate. Proverbs 9:17,18 says, *"Stolen waters are sweet, and bread eaten in secret is pleasant. But he knoweth not that the dead are there; and that her guests are in the depths of hell."* Stolen waters are of secrets is what is literally meant. God wrote that in His Word to protect us.

The false draws and seduces. The word "seduce" means to persuade to disobedience; to persuade to disloyalty; to lead astray; to entice a person to unchastity. The enemy does not tell you that death is there. He deceives one into believing that the stolen waters are sweet.

The entire ninth chapter of Proverbs compares wisdom with someone being drawn into sin by another. It shows the greatness of wisdom over sin. If God is our secret place, it results in life, light, love, peace, and joy, but if anything else is our secret place, then it results in its measure, death and hell.

"Let us hear the conclusion of the whole matter: Fear God, and keep his commandments: for this is the whole duty of man. For God shall bring every work into judgment, with every secret thing, whether it be good, or whether it be evil" (Ecclesiastes 12:13-14). The word *"fear"* in Hebrew literally means worship.

"Worship God, and keep His commandments: for this is the whole duty of man." Jesus supported this in the New Testament in Luke 4:8, when He was quoting from Deuteronomy 6:13, *"Thou shalt fear the Lord thy God...."*

Worshipping God and keeping His commandments is not grievous or burdensome. When you worship God, His commandments will be easy to observe. Worshipping God, especially in the secret place, makes keeping His commandments so easy. For God shall bring every work into judgment with every secret thing, whether it be good or evil. The whole story of Ecclesiastes is that nothing is worth anything, but God Almighty, Himself, and His commandments. That is wisdom.

Cleansing in the Secret Place

The fear of the Lord is clean, enduring for ever: the judgments of the Lord are true and righteous altogether.

More to be desired are they than gold, yea, than much fine gold: sweeter also than honey and the honeycomb.

Moreover by them is thy servant warned: and in keeping of them there is great reward.

Who can understand his errors? cleanse thou me from secret faults.

Keep back thy servant also from presumptuous sins; let them not have dominion over me: then shall I be upright, and I shall be innocent from the great transgression.

Let the words of my mouth, and the meditation of my heart, be acceptable in thy sight, O Lord, my strength, and my redeemer.

Psalm 19:9-14

The secret place of God is not something to be feared, but it is something to be desired. The question is: Do we want to live the life that is sweeter than the honeycomb? Do we want to? Do we will to do it?

It is not determined by anything but God being our secret place, and the things we do in secret, and the fact that they can be done without shame in public, if God has put His hand of approval for them to be done in public.

Romans 8:26-28 gives us some vital truths relating to the secret place. It says there are occasions we do not know what to pray for as we ought. When we pray, using it like this, infirmity simply means that we do not have natural knowledge or understanding. The Holy Spirit makes intercession for us with groanings that cannot be uttered in articulate speech.

When we pray in the spirit by the Holy Spirit, He moves us into the perfect will of Almighty God. For the Holy Spirit maketh intercession for the saints according to the will of God. The Holy Spirit will also reveal our hearts to us if we allow Him to do so.

In Psalm 19:12,13, it states, *"...cleanse thou me from secret faults. Keep back thy servant also from presumptuous sins; let them not have dominion over me...."* What is He saying there? God will never do those things unless we ask Him to do them. He will not reveal it to us, cleanse us, change it, or cause them not to have dominion over us, unless we will it.

How do we get our secret place cleaned up? How do we get the secret part of us inside cleansed? There is only one way. Unless we ask Him and yield our will to Him so that these things no longer prevail over us, He will not violate our choice.

We cannot justify our private life by the fact that our ministry is doing well by outward standards. God honors our secret place that we have established as a human being, no matter what it is. In other words, He will leave it alone. He will not intervene.

Well, what about intercession and binding the god of this world who *"blinded their minds so that they believed not,"* (2 Corinthians 4:4)? What about praying for someone rebellious and expecting God to move and to change them?

When we bind the enemy, rendering him ineffective around and over them, releasing them from those spirits, we open the way for them to be in a position to see the goodness of God in order to repent. They still, however, have to ask God for themselves before there will be a change. He honors our secret place.

God is not going to call it out in public. He waits until we ask Him, *"Don't let this thing rule and reign in my life."* You and I have to desire Him to touch and to help us change those secret places that are in life. He will not do it otherwise.

When you pray, *"God, clean my secret place up; cleanse my*

inside," do you know what is going to happen? Confrontation. You are going to suddenly find things inside of you, thoughts that you do not even approve of yourself thinking. He will begin to work in your life. *"For it is God which worketh in you both to will and to do of his good pleasure"* (Philippians 2:13).

David cried out to God to not allow those secret sins to have dominion over him any longer (Psalm 19:13). He followed that plea and said, *"...then shall I be upright; and I shall be innocent from the great transgression."* He had an understanding of the order of things. Uprightness of heart is not determined by what is done in public, but what is done in the secret place.

God loves us, and His goodness is eternal. His mercy and compassion endures forever. He never fails and His faithfulness is never ending. If our secret place is cleansed, it is because we desire it to be so. We want God to become our secret place and we pursue the desires of our heart.

It has been said that the most revealing things about a person's lifestyle is found in their trash can, a relatively private place. Archaeologists sift through ancient garbage to make discoveries about past civilizations. Even more revealing, however, is the secret place, where thoughts, desires, relationships, plans, schemes, and decisions are conceived even before they manifest.

Whatever that secret place is that needs to be God, if you pray (don't ask for prayer, open the Bible and pray it yourself), God will do it. Why is He doing it? He is bringing us into a time where He wants the Spirit of liberty so much in us, around us, and about us, that there will not be one bit of bondage to hold us back from obeying Almighty God.

Chapter 3
Power of the Secret Place

The catalyst, and source of everything we do that is of eternal value, is spawned out of our knowing Him. It is interesting to note that in Matthew 16:13, Jesus asked His disciples, *"...Whom do men say that I the Son of man am?"*

Several responded to that leading question, repeating the local gossip. *"Some say you are Elias; some say you are Jeremias, some say this; some say that."* They all knew what others said about Jesus, and no doubt the rationale for such thinking. Jesus then came to the point by his next question. *"But Whom say YE that I Am?"*

Wanting to have the right answer and not disappoint the Master, their minds must have raced through all the possibilities, eliminating each one with just cause. I can visualize dumbfounded stares, and almost hear their breaths being drawn in and held in anticipation. They just did not know for themselves. One of them finally opened his mouth.

When he started speaking, the others might have thought, *"Well, it's just old Peter spouting off at the mouth again."* Risking ridicule and perhaps ostracism, Peter boldly spoke with all sincerity and said, *"...Thou art the Christ, the Son of the living God"* (Matthew 16:16).

This time Peter had it right. Jesus looked at him approvingly, and there was compassion, because He wanted Peter to be right every other time. Here at last, this beloved disciple was right on target, *"spot on"* as the South Africans would say it.

If Jesus were using modern English, His response might have been, *"Peter, flesh and blood has not revealed that to you. This kind of revelation of Who I Am to you, personally, does not come by flesh and blood. No one else can tell you Who I Am, Peter, but it comes from One only, My Father, which is in heaven. He has revealed this to you, Peter."*

Then He said something else. He told Peter that it is upon this rock, the rock of revelation of Who He is, that He will build His church. When you know Who He is through this revelation personally, then and only then, the gates of hell shall not prevail against you.

It is not just positive confessions, although they are important, or doctrines, which are also important, but Almighty God has to give the believer the revelation of Who Jesus is. When you have that revelation solid as a rock in your heart, you will push back the gates of hell. You will turn the battle back at the gates every time. Hallelujah!

Paul, who gave us one-third of the New Testament, after having said and done so much, declared, *"That I might know Him..."* (Philippians 3:10). He knew that if he kept growing in experiential knowledge and revelation of knowing Jesus, he would have more resurrection power, more glory, more strength, more ability working in him.

Everything that we are and do that counts for Him, is from having a personal revelation of the Lord Jesus Christ. That is why Paul knew it was not his might or power, but the faith in the Name of the Lord Jesus Christ. When you know Him, you do not have a problem with faith. It takes a revelation of Jesus as the Christ.

Understanding the power of the secret place, we will be put in a position to know Him, so that the gates of hell shall not prevail against us. We will be used to turn back the battle at the gate. Every time the enemy shows up at the gate, we will turn the battle back because we know the Lord.

Knowing Him will cause you to stand when all other people fail you. Knowing Him will cause you to stand when persecution comes and men say all manner of evil against you. Knowing Him will cause you to have your feet firmly planted on the solid rock.

You will not be moved; you will not be swayed. From the moment that Peter said, *"Thou art the Christ, the Son of the living God,"* he was changed from a reed blowing in the wind to a rock. It effectually happened on the day of Pentecost. We have had Pentecost, have we not? We should have a revelation of the Lord Jesus Christ.

Knowing Him will absolutely defeat the "Nimrod" spirit. Nimrod, who founded Babylon, was a mighty hunter, the father of humanism, selfishness, and egotism. He subscribed to the idea of exalting one's self up against Almighty God and His decrees.

When you know Jesus the Christ, it will destroy the rebellious, humanistic "Nimrod" spirit. It will become evident that all flesh is as grass, and is going to wither away, but only that which is of the spirit realm is eternal.

Promises of the Secret Place

God has shown us that the secret place is powerful. If we will work it to our advantage, that power will absolutely change us into what He has prophesied and promised. A careful look at Psalm 91 will reveal powerful promises.

> **He that dwelleth in the secret place of the most High shall abide under the shadow of the Almighty.**
>
> **I will say of the Lord, He is my refuge and my fortress: my God; in him will I trust.**
>
> **Surely he shall deliver thee from the snare of the fowler, and from the noisome pestilence.**
>
> **He shall cover thee with his feathers, and under his wings shalt thou trust: his truth shall be thy shield and buckler.**
>
> **Thou shalt not be afraid for the terror by night; nor for the arrow that flieth by day;**

Nor for the pestilence that walketh in darkness; nor for the destruction that wasteth at noonday.

A thousand shall fall at thy side, and ten thousand at thy right hand; but it shall not come nigh thee.

Only with thine eyes shalt thou behold and see the reward of the wicked.

Because thou hast made the Lord, which is my refuge, even the most High, thy habitation;

There shall no evil befall thee, neither shall any plague come nigh thy dwelling.

For he shall give his angels charge over thee, to keep thee in all thy ways.

They shall bear thee up in their hands, lest thou dash thy foot against a stone.

Thou shalt tread upon the lion and adder: the young lion and the dragon shalt thou trample under feet.

Because he hath set his love upon me, therefore will I deliver him: I will set him on high, because he hath known my name.

He shall call upon me, and I will answer him: I will be with him in trouble; I will deliver him, and honour him.

With long life will I satisfy him, and show him my salvation.

Psalm 91

Every promise in Psalm 91 is contingent on the first few words, *"He that dwelleth in the secret place of the most High...."* What is the secret place of the most High, so that we can dwell there and have all of these promises manifested in our lives?

The secret place is that which you consider the top priority in your life. The secret place is where nobody else is with you to tell you what you may or may not do, speak, see, hear, or touch. In the secret place, you will do what is in the abundance of your heart.

This is the most powerful place of your life. Jesus indicated in Matthew 6:1-6, that if your private and public lives are inconsistent, you are a hypocrite. If in public is the only place you prophesy, give tongues and interpretations, shout, dance, jump, clap, pray, or study the Word, you make a pretense of all of that. In so doing, you open up yourself to familiar spirits, who have one motive behind them, that is, to be seen and heard.

What some people are doing in their secret place is stealing from them, killing, destroying, tormenting, oppressing and depressing them. How free do you want to be? We are as free as what we do in secret.

Cheating on income tax, cheating on a spouse, nipping at a bottle or other unmentionable substances, gambling even legally, looking at questionable television, pornography in all forms, or languishing in a recliner, are all activities done in a private place. Who does it glorify?

Even wholesome activities can crowd out God. Spending time with the family or enjoying recreational activities are important in a well-balanced individual, but even these essentials can become your god.

If your all consuming top priority of life is golfing, your job, getting the kids through college, operating your ministry, it will become your master. Perhaps the priority in your mind is to go fishing instead of, *"I have got to have time to be with God."* *Remember* your top priority in your secret place controls, governs, and becomes authority in your life.

Can you know that your secret place is God? You know when you cannot survive unless you have time alone with God. You cannot survive unless you read His Word. You will know that God is your secret place and you are dwelling there when your number one drive, desire, and motivation force in life is to spend time alone with God.

This time is not lengthy, solitary confinement. Jesus went up on the Mount of Transfiguration and was transformed. His disciples wanted to build three tabernacles. Jesus said in essence, *"No, we are going down off the mountain;*

we have experienced this for one reason only: we are to go down and minister to the people."

The first thing He did after that, was cast out devils. Isolation is a trick of the devil. People sometimes get into a religious mode, thinking they are going to purge themselves by isolation. You can call them six months later, and they are still in the prayer closet believing God is still purging and purifying them. That is not God. His way is to eliminate the problem, get blessed, then go out and minister to people.

Nevertheless, Jesus withdrew regularly to keep His time with the Father consistent. How much time do you have to spend for it to be the secret place? Start where you are *every* day. It is not quantity, it is quality. As you begin with a few minutes daily, it will grow and expand. You will find that you take advantage of every spare moment of time to draw nigh unto God, to get into Him.

Concealed and Hidden

The word "secret" has shades of meaning, connotations and denotations. First of all, it means *"concealed,"* which usually indicates a premeditated hiding of something from someone. It is not done coincidentally.

We conceal things for a number of reasons. We may withhold something to be revealed at a later time, the thing may require privacy or confidentiality, or because shame is connected with the object or deed. In any case, concealing is an intentional act.

Things are hidden by us for the same reasons as concealment, but it also can indicate someone wanting to protect a treasure. People want to pray with me, but they will never see me praying like I do in my secret place. To me, prayer of that quality and dimension is so intimate, that I do not want anybody else there for any reason.

If I want to weep before God, I want to weep without people wondering what is falling apart. If I want to jump, I do not want somebody saying that it is not for today. I want to be in a position praying in the Holy Ghost, or commanding and decreeing the Word, without having to justify to flesh.

I have never agreed with people saying that you cannot tell your Daddy (Abba), God, everything that is bothering you. When I go into my prayer closet and I put the blood of Jesus on it, that door is closed to the devil.

I want to be in a position that if God, the Holy Spirit, wants to groan through me, I don't have to defend that as a cunning devised fable to anybody. If He wants to travail through me, I don't want somebody arguing with me that it is a metaphor and should not be done.

When I am at home in my secret place, familiar spirits are not going to use me, because nobody is going to get the glory but God. There are just some things that need to be private. It seems like we are forever wanting to expose that which needs to be private, and make private that which needs exposure.

Council and Counsel

Secret is frequently connected with activities of a council. A city council is a political governing body. Even though council meetings occur in public, we know that the inner workings of government are most often done through lobbying and discussion behind closed doors.

What you and I do in secret becomes the council of our lives. It becomes the governing body and controlling power of our lives. It is the law-making body of our lives, where decisions about justice, ethics, and morality are made. If our secret place is God, then He will become our ruling power.

What we do in secret begins to counsel, direct, and shape our thinking. It begins to formulate how we hear. It becomes our motivation. If God is our council, He is our secret place, then He becomes our counselor.

Covered

Secret also means covered, similar to concealed or hidden. What you do in secret, covers you. We all have experi-

enced times when we have come across someone and everything seemed right, but something inside said, *"It's not
kosher."* You might have even rebuked yourself for being
judgmental and critical, only to find out later, if there was no
repentance, that what they were doing in secret was wrong.

Everything seemed right and looked right, but there was
an intuitive knowing that all was not as it appeared. What
you do in secret becomes your covering.

In Acts, chapter four, when Peter and John performed
that notable miracle by the power of God, the onlookers
remarked that they were ignorant and unlearned men. They
also took note that they had been with Jesus. Peter and John
were covered with Jesus.

*"He that dwelleth in the secret place of the most High shall
abide under the shadow (the covering) of the Almighty."* By the
shadow of Peter, signs and wonders took place. It was not
Peter at all, but what he was doing in the secret place. You are
covered with what you are doing in your secret place.

In Numbers, chapter 13, Moses sent out 12 spies to the
land that flowed with milk and honey. They brought back
that enormous cluster of grapes hanging down on a pole,
which was so tremendous that it had to be carried on the
shoulders of two men.

The ten spies, the majority (so much for majority rule in
spiritual matters), reported that there were giants in that land.
They saw themselves as grasshoppers and it influenced their
decision. We see ourselves inside, where nobody knows, and
it too influences what we decide to do. We must see ourselves
in the image of God, because He sees us that way.

Joshua and Caleb were of another spirit, the spirit of
faith. They knew that if God said it, that was all that mat-
tered. In Numbers 14:9, they said, *"Only rebel not ye against
the Lord, neither fear ye the people of the land; for they are bread for
us: their defense is departed from them, and the Lord is with us:
fear them not."*

In Hebrew, when it says, *"their defense is departed from*

them," it literally means, *"their shadow is departed from them."* The shadow is Almighty God, and He is not with them. When we dwell in the secret place, the most High, we shall abide under the shadow of the Almighty. The Almighty there is *El Shaddai,* the one pouring out every blessing upon us.

Wonder and Mystery

Secrets are full of wonder. What you do in secret becomes wonderful to you. Adulterous affairs, unwholesome television, wrong relationships, anything that is done in the secret place, becomes wonderful to you.

If you seek God and fellowship with Him in the secret place, He will become more and more wonderful to you. If you study and meditate the Word of God in secret, the Word will be wonderful to you. You will have a capacity for understanding the Word that others, who do not spend time with it, do not have.

Things good or evil done in secret become wonderful to people. God desires to be your secret place so He can become wonderful to you.

Secrets are also mysterious. After having been exposed, people who are involved in wrongdoing will frequently say, *"I don't know what made me do it."* Their secret doings had become a mystery even to them. They become so entangled, it becomes difficult to sort out the facts.

The positive side of secrets being mysterious is that, if we seek God and delight in Him in the secret place, Jesus Christ, the mystery, the hope of glory, will become much more so the hope of glory in our lives.

El Elyon

"He that dwelleth in the secret place of the most High." The words *"most High,"* is El Elyon in Hebrew, which is the same word used in Genesis, chapter 14, when Abram said, *"...I have lift up mine hand unto the Lord, the most high God, the possessor of heaven and earth, That I will not take from a thread even to a*

shoelatchet, and that I will not take any thing that is thine, lest thou shouldest say, I have made Abram rich" (Genesis 14:22,23). It is God in His creative power, blessing you with all that you need in your life.

The same principle is in John 14:13, when Jesus said, *"And whatsoever ye shall ask in my name, that will I do, that the Father may be glorified in the Son."* It means that if you ask for it, providing of course that it does not violate God's will, and it doesn't exist, He will create it for you. That is El Elyon!

Who then, do you run to when you need help? Who do you run to when you need assurance and blessing? Do you run to the nearest prayer place? Do you run to everybody else, or do you run to the most High God? Do you run to your secret place and just tell Daddy all about it? Do you run to Him? If you do, then you are going to see His mighty fortress, His *"hedge of protection."*

Who do you run to for protection? Do you get your .45 caliber automatic weapon? People will not go where God wants them to go and do because they are afraid. When you dwell in the secret place of the most High, you will know that Almighty God, El Elyon, is your fortress, is your hedge of protection, and He is an impenetrable fortress through which no one can invade.

When something tries to come against you, who do you trust? Your confidence is in the one who you perceive to be a fortress, one who has strength and protection. When you go to God, you will be secure, without fear. That means when He says, "Go," you will go in confidence. When He says, "Do," you will do with total security, and you will be without fear.

Translations besides the King James Version, further amplify the first verse of Psalm 91 indicating the place of safety in the shadow of the Almighty. Other translations taken from The Bible from 26 Translations read as follow:

Whoso dwelleth under the defence of the Most High, shall abide under the shadow of the Almighty — PBV

He who dwelleth under the protection of the Most High shall lodge in the shelter of the God of heaven — Sept

He who lives in the secret shelter of the Most High lodges in the shadow of the Almighty — Ber

He who lives as a ward of the Most High shall repose under the protection of the Almighty — Har

He who dwells in the secret place of the Most High shall remain stable and fixed under the shadow of the Almighty [Whose power no foe can withstand] — Amp

He who dwells under the shelter of the Most High, who abides under the shadow of the Almighty — AAT

The secret place of the Most High, the shadow of the Almighty, is the giver, the provider, the all-supplier of every need. When He is your secret place, He shall *"cover thee with His feathers."*

There is a true story that illustrates this point graphically. In a certain city, there was a rash of torture and rapes perpetrated on young women. A young university student had just newly been born again, and therefore, did not have a solid command of the Word of God. She left school one night walking alone to her car in a darkened parking lot.

Sure enough, when she got to her car, the rapist was there. He grabbed her and panic gripped her. Realizing that she had no one else to turn to, she knew that her only way of escape was God Almighty. Struggling to fight off the rapist, she knew he was gaining control.

Suddenly she remembered a sermon her pastor preached from Psalm 91. All she could remember from the sermon was the word "feathers." At the top of her voice, she started screaming *"Feathers! Feathers! Feathers!"* The rapist got so shook up that he took off. When God is your secret place, even if all you can think of is "feathers," it is enough! Hallelujah!

We should be ever growing in faith and understanding that the power of life and death is in our tongue. That which we speak is bringing forth life or death. We should know how to call those things that be not as though they were. We should know our authority and dominion.

We have to understand too, that if it is not more than head knowledge, it will be a detriment rather than faith. Faith in a nutshell, is simply trusting God as a child, believing He is going to do what He said He would do. Jesus said, *"...Except ye be converted, and become as little children, ye shall not enter into the kingdom of heaven"* (Matthew 18:3).

Even in all the dominion and authority, we must be as little children before God. The reason many are not receiving the blessings of the kingdom of heaven, is because they are not like a little child with God. We must never outgrow being a child before God.

When God is your secret place every day of your life, you become invincible, not in your own strength, but in His might. When you awaken, the devil has to say, *"Oh no! He's up again!"* because you walk in the protection of El Elyon, the most High God.

Chapter 4
Deliverance in the Secret Place

A few years ago I said to God, *"Look at this generation, Father. We are seemingly weak. And you know what we have been going through."* He answered me saying, *"That's all right. In your weakness, I Am made strong."* And He began to unfold to me the fact that every person that had been mighty on the face of the earth in the Name of the Lord Jesus Christ, had either known their weakness, or like Moses, who spent forty years on the back side of the desert, learned that they are weak without Him.

He said, *"I take the foolish things of the world to confound the wise. I'm going to take the weak things of the world to confound the strong. I'm going to take the ignorant things to confound the wise."*

Count It All Joy

Many of you have been going through things that would be called temptations, tests, or trials. God says to *"Count it all joy."* A current way to say it might be, *"Throw a party!"* When you are going through temptations, tests, and trials, just throw a party. Once Milton and I were on the road and I called home about something and talked to our oldest son. I said, *"John, how are things going? What's happening at the church, and so forth?"*

He replied, *"We are throwing a party. We are having a count-it-all-joy party."*

I said, *"Glory to God!"* and hung up the phone.

Milton asked, *"What's going on?"*

51

I replied, *"They are having a count-it-all-joy party."*

"How would you have such a party?" he asked.

I answered, *"I don't know, but I believe the Holy Ghost knows how to have a count-it-all-joy party."* It may seem foolish, but it works.

A couple had not been able to sell a home for quite a long time. They learned that when you go through temptations, tests, and trials, to count it all joy. They called their friends, brought them to the home, and had a party that exceeded all parties. The very next day that home was sold, to the glory of God. When things are not moving, throw a party. It could be a hallelujah party just between you and God.

People did not invite Jesus to their functions because His face was sour and hanging on the ground. When He arrived on the scene, a party began to happen with great exceeding joy. It is time for us to realize that the prodigal son, the church of the Lord Jesus Christ, has come home, and we are to throw a party to the glory of God.

Put a ring on your finger. You are married to the King of kings and the Lord of lords. Put a robe on your back, for you are royalty. Put shoes on your feet; you are not a slave. Then set your feet to dancing, and eat at the Master's table. *"Thou preparest a table before me in the presence of mine enemies..."* (Psalm 23:5). This means that the Lord has prepared a feast for me where I can sit, dine, and just look on while He, the Lord, the Captain of the army, the Lord of warfare, the Lord of hosts, Jehovah Nissi, fights my battles for me. Hallelujah!

Spirit of Might

The body of Christ needs to be assured that the church is not going under, but rather, it is going over and all the way up. All of those Bible greats like David, Moses, Abraham, and the rest, knew that they could do nothing of themselves. Like with Gideon, God just says, *"Thou mighty man of valor, I'm going to cause my Holy Spirit to clothe Himself upon you to control you and to possess you, and you are going to win the victory against every impossible odd that you face."*

Philippians 2:13 says, *"For it is God which worketh in you both to will and to do of his good pleasure."* In the next verse, it tells us to do it all *without* murmuring or complaining against God or anyone else. We are learning to know what it is to see beyond faults, needs, circumstances, and situations. We are learning to lift our heads up to behold the Author and Finisher of our faith, knowing that He is the Alpha and Omega, the beginning and the end, and everything in between. He has never failed within a generation, nor any person, and He is not going to fail with you and me.

God is pouring out of that spirit of might upon His people. It is grace, of course. He is pouring out sufficiency and strength. Grace is help, sufficiency, ability, efficiency, strength, might, and power. It is the Holy Spirit, Himself (Zechariah 12:10; Hebrews 10:29). He has given us the grace. He says in 1 Peter 4:10, *"There are manifold graces."*

Scripture tells us there is one grace that can put us in a position for God to make all grace abound toward us. It is revealed in 2 Corinthians, chapters 8 and 9. This is the grace of giving and Paul exhorts, *"...see that ye abound in this grace also"* (2 Corinthians 8:7). We are going to need the spirit of might in these days. We are going to need to proclaim Psalm 103:1, *"Bless the Lord, O my soul: and all that is within me, bless his holy name."*

Further on in verse 5, it says, *"Who satisfieth my mouth with good things; so that my youth is renewed like the eagle's."* You are not just getting older; you are getting wiser. You are not getting weaker; you are getting stronger. We are going to run the race and finish. We have received a spirit of might. We are to receive the manifold graces that are necessary to function.

If you fall when you are running with the legs of a man, how will you keep up with the legs of a horse? The closer you get to the speed of light, the faster you go. We are getting closer to the light of the world, the Lord Jesus Christ, Who is coming again soon. We are going to speed up in running the race and finishing our course.

You will find out that your body does not need twenty hours of sleep every night, and you can miss a meal and still survive. You can stand and be found faithful to Almighty God. He restores our youth like an eagle's. He gives the spirit of might. It was said of Moses that his strength was not abated, and his eyes did not grow dim (Deuteronomy 34:7). Receive that anointing. Muscles atrophy when they are not moved. I am going to function in spirit, soul, and body, as I have never functioned before because God, the Holy Spirit, is giving me the *"unction for the gumption to function."* It is religion alone that sits up with the dead, and we are not baby-sitting the dead. Hallelujah!

Having Done All To Stand, Stand

It has already been established that the promises of Psalm 91 are conditional on those first few words, *"He that dwelleth in the secret place of the most High...."* This tells us why some people repeatedly confess Psalm 91 from head knowledge, and it amounts to no more than chanting montras as they do in Eastern religions. Jesus called it *"...vain repetitions as the heathens do..."* (Matthew 6:7).

Just repeating things like, *"He has given His angels charge over me to keep me in all of my ways, to bear me up on their wings so that I will not dash my foot against a stone. I will not stumble or fall. A thousand may fall at my left side and ten thousand at my right side..."* without something happening in the rest of your being is just not enough. This is the number one place that the enemy will tempt, test, and try to defeat you.

When an illness attacks like AIDS or cancer, all of a sudden you turn to the saints and the church elders to pray for you. The devil is quick to point out to you, Aunt So-and-So did all of that, and she was saintly, but she went on to be with Jesus; or Brother So-and-So was not healed of AIDS even though he confessed the Word continuously. He whispers to you, *"What makes you think that you are going to be healed and delivered from cancer or AIDS?"* This is how the battle rages in your mind. However, when God is your secret place, you will run into that place for protection. You will confide in God, and you will stand your ground.

Having done all to stand, you will stand (Ephesians 6:13,14). This means you have done everything you know to do, and then stand. There is however, more meaning. It also means *"to have no passage through."*

When my children were young, they liked to watch the cartoons on Saturday mornings. One particular character was interesting. It was a roadrunner, a speedy bird. That roadrunner would be going at full steam, and he was always on a dusty road. Everywhere he went, the dust would fly behind him. As he was leaving a cloud of dust, he would make sounds like, *"Be-beep, be-beep, be-beep."* He was determined to overcome everything in his way, but he would get to a certain point, and there would be an insurmountable obstacle in his way. Then he would just screech to a halt, and his *"be-beep"* would fade away.

The enemy comes at the Christian, having done all to stand, knowing his authority in Christ Jesus; knowing his secret place; knowing who he is in Him. That devil starts to *"be-beep"* with cancer, *"be-beep"* with a threat of bankruptcy, *"be-beep"* with a threat of divorce, *"be-beep"* with AIDS, or whatever else he has, and that Christian is still standing. He hears the *"be-beep"* of the devil coming as hard as he can at him, and his feet dig up the dust, but at last the *"be-beep"* just fades away. Hallelujah!

Here is where you say that God is the most High, your secret place, and *"A thousand may fall at my left side and ten thousand may fall at my right side, but it shall not come nigh me."* When God is your secret place, that is exactly the kind of lifestyle you will have. The Bible says, *"Many are the afflictions of the righteous..."* (Psalm 34:19). We do not have to invite them, but it further says, *"...but the Lord delivereth him out of them all."*

Hinds' Feet

Psalm 91:14 says that deliverance comes, *"Because he has set his love upon me...."* It is indicative of a relationship established on trust, allowing God to be our secret place. How do you know He is your secret place? You desire and pursue Him; you hunger and thirst for Him, His Word and His presence in prayer, communion, praise, worship, and fellowship with Him alone. That is how He becomes your first love. That is how your Christianity does not become dull, boring, or flaky. It is always fresh and alive.

He says, *"Because you have set your first love upon Me,"* meaning the deepest affection, *"I will deliver you."* He continues to say that He will also set us on high. God's way is not just to bring us out some way, somehow, but it is Joel 2:25, *"To restore all that the locust, the cankerworm, the caterpillar, and the palmerworm has eaten!"* God's way says that no matter what, *"I can do all things through Jesus Christ,"* because He is constantly infusing me with His strength that is beyond my own strength.

God's way is not to just deliver us, or for us to walk around Mount Sinai one more time in the wilderness. His way is to set us on high. What happens when we are set on high? We are not depressed, discouraged, defeated, or down. We are set up over circumstances, and we are ruling over them. The throne of the servant is over that which is opposing him.

He will give us *"hinds' feet"* so that we can run on rough places, crazy places, and hard places. We will have the swiftness to run right over them. It is the anointing. Jesus is set in heavenly places at the right hand of God, the Almighty Father, and according to Ephesians 1:3, God has *"blessed us with all spiritual blessings in heavenly places in Christ."*

Psalm 91:15 says, *"He shall call upon me and I will answer him...."* How shall I call upon Him? When do you call upon Him? You call on Him every time you have a need. You call upon Him every time you need comfort, because you are receiving affliction or persecution. He says,

56

"Let the afflicted pray; let the afflicted call upon him" (James 5:13). He did *not* say to let them call on everybody else to do their praying for them. If you are afflicted, get on your face and call on Him yourself.

What does it mean to be afflicted? It means you are not understood. It does not make a difference whether you are Asian, Black, White, Male, or Female. The devil does not come against you with persecution because of your color, race, or gender. His evil works come because the Word is in you, and it comes to immediately steal the Word.

Sometimes you are not going to have time to flip out your formula card on fifteen steps to prayer. In December, 1969, after being recently baptized in the Holy Ghost, Milton and I, with our two sons, were traveling northeast of Atlanta on I-85 from Columbus to Toccoa, Georgia. It was about 9:30 at night, when suddenly the weather changed. The wind started blowing furiously and rain came down in torrents. Both children were asleep, one on my lap, and the other on the back seat. Without warning, the car tilted up and over on its side, and we found ourselves flying on one right front wheel. Milton looked over toward me and said, *"I have no control over the automobile."*

As we peered through sloshing wiper blades, we saw a cement wall and embankment ahead where an overpass crossed the road. We were heading directly for it. I looked at the speedometer and it read a startling 82 miles per hour. We knew that at any moment we all would be splattered into splinters. This all happened in seconds and there was no time to think.

I was so ignorant, I could hardly recite John 3:16, but all of a sudden my mouth opened and blurted out, *"JESUS!"* At that moment, we were right at the point of impact, when the car came down on four wheels, and we drove safely under the overpass. Hallelujah!

When we came through on the other side, the car was picked up on the right wheel by the force of the powerful wind, and again we were in peril. We headed for a road sign, and then ran it over like it was a match stick. As we were fly-ing toward the embankment, I remember thinking that if we hit it, we wouldn't even be a grease spot. There would be nothing left of us.

We careened down the embankment, which at that moment looked like the Grand Canyon. Once again, I shout-ed,"*JESUS!*" The whole car lit up. It was like a giant hand came on the front end of that car and stopped it on the embankment. I shouted, "*Jesus did it! Jesus did it!*" Milton looked at me and said, "*I know Jesus did it,*" as if to say, "*Enough already, would you please shut up.*"

He climbed out to examine the situation. The wheels were stopped right on the edge of that culvert. As Milton climbed back in the car, we both thought that we would need a tow truck to pull us out of there. Milton cranked that car up, put it into reverse, and backed it out like we were on a dry street instead of a wet grassy embankment.

It did not matter that I had been in church every time the door opened, or that I taught Sunday School, or that I played the organ in church. The fact is, at that time I did not know about angels, or about Psalm 91. What it took was, "*JESUS*" from the heart level. "*He shall call upon me, and I will answer him...*" (Psalm 91:15).

Point of No Return

The next words are, "*...I will be with him in trouble....*" David said, in Psalm 139:8, "*...if I make my bed in hell, thou art there....*" The Holy Spirit is present everywhere. In essence, the Lord is saying, "*I will be with you in trouble. If you want out of it, I will deliver you.*"

The enemy knows how to get at each one of us. Most people have not slept in the places I have had to, or eaten what I have been required to eat because of the nature of the ministry the Lord has given me. This is not to boast in pride or even to evoke sympathy, but it is just simply fact.

One bed was so filthy, I had to lay my robe on it and not move all night so that I could stay clean. I have also been in huts that most people could not even imagine. As Paul, I know how to be content in all things. I know how to be abased and how to abound.

There was a time when it seemed like whenever we would go to a hotel, they would put us in the worst room available. When you spend three and sometimes four weeks every month in hotels, you become quite a connoisseur in that area. My face would be smiling, but inside a volcano would be brewing because the hotel would not provide what I knew I should have.

The point of no return came during one of my trips to Jamaica, where the hotel management was being dishonest and refused to give me the room to which I was entitled by arrangement. After speaking to the desk attendants to no avail, I decided, *"This is the last time any hotel will ever upset me again as long as I am in this life."* I did not realize it then, but I had made an unconditional decision from which there was no return.

Since that time, no matter where I have had to stay, I have not been moved or upset, regardless of the circumstances. When I made a *"point of no return"* decision, God worked His character in me so that now the enemy cannot use hotels to get to me. When you finally want to come out of trouble, out of feeling sorry for yourself, He will deliver you, but only if you make that all important decision from which there is no return.

Most people do not think of God being in places where there is activity going on that is shall we say, *"less than reputable."* He is certainly not a part of dope-shooting, lying, cheating, stealing, violent crimes, or gossiping, yet He is everywhere. God is the ultimate "Good Samaritan." When His people get to the *point of no return* and make the decision that they want out of trouble, He is there to deliver them.

God told Ezekiel to prophesy to the wind. You may just be a bag of wind now, but in God's sight you are a warrior. He will take what you speak out, deposit that which you need, and cause you to walk as the warrior that you are, instead of the wimp that you might have been.

Who is going to come in the gates? We have enemies at the gate (place of authority), but the promise of God is that we shall turn every battle back at the gate (Isaiah 28:6). We shall possess the gates of our enemies (Genesis 22:17). When there are things in us that are contrary to the obedience of Jesus Christ, and we decide that it cannot continue, who do you think will come into the gates? *"Lift up your heads, O ye gates; even lift them up, ye everlasting doors; and the King of glory shall come in"* (Psalm 24:9). Who is this King? It is the Lord of hosts, the Lord of warfare. You are in His army, and He will deliver His warriors.

The Lord goes on to say even more than that. He will not only deliver you, but He will *honor* you. James 2:13 in the New International Version says, *"...Mercy triumphs over judgment."* If you will show your persecutors and accusers mercy, your mercy will triumph over their judgment of you. You will come out winning.

Satisfaction in Long Life

If your life is anything but satisfying, He is not your first love. When Jesus is your first love, you will come to places of growth and learn to be content in any and all things. You will be able to fight battles and overcome hurts. All of us have weak spots and know what it is like to be challenged or wounded. We must also know to run to the secret place and say, *"Jesus, I'm hurt. I'm tempted to be offended. I confess the weakness of myself. Comfort me, Holy Spirit."*

We are coming into the glory of the resurrection power that sets our hinds' feet on our high places (Psalm 18:33). God's people have to get right with Him in the secret places. The church of America of late has experienced some disgrace and has been without honor. However, God says, *"I will not only deliver that church, people, or individual, but I will also honor them, and to that I will add length of days. With long life will I satisfy them."* God is ready to honor us but we are going to have to set our affection on Him.

God must be my everything. He is the length of my days, and He will satisfy me. It is not boring or dissatisfying to live for Jesus. Nothing quite satisfies like God. No amount of money, position, knowing celebrities, substance, or habit will satisfy you like getting alone with God and drinking living water at the unbroken cistern.

If you want long life, then make God your secret place. Only God knows how much each of us needs to be honored. If you live a godly life, you will suffer persecution. If you don't need to be honored for any other reason, you need to be honored above the persecution that is coming against you. That is why the secret place is important to us.

The Quick Fix

Most of the *"deliverance"* in the United States, that I have seen and heard, has involved people trying to cast out works of flesh. They can never be cast out, so they just magnify and increase.

Nobody is able to cast out works of the flesh. The only way the works of the flesh will not be in control, is to walk in the spirit, that is, to obey the Word of God by the power of the Holy Spirit residing in us. Many would rather have a "quick fix," but it just does not happen that way. It happens by daily building the character of God in your life. We build the character of God into our life by daily choosing to be doers of the Word.

Jesus is not ignorant of our temptations, tests and trials. He was tempted with every temptation possible to humanity. The only difference between Him and the rest of humanity is that He refused every temptation. However, because He lived as a man on earth, and suffered the same things that we encounter, through Him we have the ability to resist the enemy also.

The darkness of the secret place of your life is being challenged. As you yield your will and say as Jesus did, *"Not my will, Lord, but Yours be done,"* you walk in His strength and ability. When you allow the cross to be planted into your darkness, and the blood of the Lord Jesus Christ to wash, penetrate, and cleanse that darkness, the resurrection life, power, and glory comes.

"...Every, plant which my heavenly Father hath not planted shall be rooted up" (Matthew 15:13). Whatever is not planted by God, He uproots. He is trying to uproot every ungodly and unholy thing in our lives, including aims, attitudes, purposes, and motives. If we allow Him to clean the secret place of our lives, the host of heaven will go to battle on our behalf for every dream, vision, hope, and desire for our lives that is pure, because they obey the voice of the Word. God is indeed trying to save our lives.

Chapter 5
Power of Secret Deeds

We are at the point of time for a new season of the Lord. In recent years, it has been evident that God has been moving on the church to get out of emotional dependency on one another, and back to a position of being totally dependent on Almighty God. He is the one that we must depend on and trust in the priority realm.

If every day, we wake up in anticipation and excitement about walking with the Lord, we will not come to the end of the day disappointed. Just to walk with the Lord is enough. Just to experience His presence is enough. We will be right on time for all that we are to do. He is bringing us to the reality that He is doing something new each day.

God is bringing us to the understanding that nothing that we can experience in the sense realm, or possess, is worth anything when compared to knowing Him. As Paul wrote in Philippians 3:8, *"...I count all things but loss for the excellency of the knowledge of Christ Jesus my Lord..."*, and then in verse 10 he continues to say, *"That I may know him, and the power of his resurrection...."*

Too Busy For God

Many excuse themselves from the intimate knowledge of God because they are just too busy. It is purely deception by the enemy. How in the world are we going to survive as the body of Christ without the kind of secret place that is spoken of in the Word? If Jesus needed to draw apart with God to be alone with Him in the secret place, it is absolutely vital for us to do no less.

Jesus says, in John 5:44, that if you seek honor and glory from men rather than from God, your faith will not work. This is why faith is not working for some people. They won't do anything unless they know it is going to please someone. This is a part of the work of the secret place, that is, to work the character of God in us that is desirable to Him.

It is hard on the flesh to pursue the primary goal of one day standing before the Master and hearing Him say, *"Well done, thou good and faithful servant."* The number one thing that has to matter, even if the whole world turns against you, is knowing in the deep recesses of your heart, that you have heard from God, are pleasing Him, and you belong to nobody else. You can trust God when you are wrong, knowing that He is big enough to straighten you out because you belong to Him. First John 1:9 is the path of this goal.

Absolute Honesty

When I was ministering in the Natal Province of South Africa, I was in a congregation of Indian people whose ancestors settled in South Africa generations ago. Along with me besides the Indian pastor, was my daughter-in-law, Glenda, an evangelist to the Zulu people, and also an elderly man, Charles Neilson, who had ministered with past men of renown in Pentecostal circles like David duPlessis, John G. Lake, Smith Wigglesworth, and William Branham.

The service that night was powerful, and I was used as a vessel to minister tremendous prophecy by the Holy Spirit. Brother Neilson even remarked to me, *"Sister, I am going to pray that God will use you to prophesy like that everywhere He sends you,"* and this was a man who has seen much in seventy-four years. To God be the glory!

God was not finished with that service, however, and words of knowledge came forth, as well as many healings. However, there was a young Indian lady in a wheelchair. When I asked her what was wrong with her, she said that she was paralyzed from the waist down due to an automobile accident. We laid hands on her, everybody prayed, but nothing happened.

At this point, I must note that there are numerous gods worshipped in India. To many of them, Jesus is just another one to add to the roll call. Some will even put a cross in their homes along with the other idols to be venerated with incense.

This particular young lady was wearing string bracelets on her right wrist. Brother Neilson, a seasoned veteran, began to talk to her and she admitted going to what we would call a witch doctor. He had put the bracelets on her for healing after praying to some devils. I saw a string around her neck, and gently slid it out of her blouse. On the end of it was an amulet, which we found out was also put on her by a witch doctor.

At first she did not want to admit the truth about the amulets, but then she finally did. Brother Neilson asked her to remove them, but she was in such fear that she just refused to take them off. He very lovingly told her, *"Until you choose Jesus, and deny the god that put those things on you and repent, you will not walk out of that wheelchair. You will not be healed."* He then turned to the Indian pastor and asked him to visit her and minister to her that following week, to which the pastor agreed.

Many have pretended that things did not happen when something was not right, and should have had the boldness to say, *"Get your life right, then you will receive blessing."* If Brother Neilson had not been honest with that woman, the people would have thought God did not heal her. The power of God was there to heal her, but she was double-minded between two opinions. She had not made the decision of whom she would serve.

If we are truly seeking to get people saved, healed, delivered, and set on the path of righteousness, we are going to have to be absolutely honest with the Holy Spirit, doing what He says to do, saying what He tells us to say, and believing without reservations. This is part of the equipment for this move of God. We must get beyond seeking the glory and honor of man, and get to the place of desiring God's glory and honor alone. Then our faith will work, we will please Him, and He will reward us openly.

It does not come without much dying to the flesh. You find that there are more layers to the onion than you ever thought possible, and you cry with every layer being stripped off. We have seen where Jesus said that when you are just seeking the praise of men, your faith will not work. Some want miracles, signs, and wonders to obtain the approval of men or to make themselves appear more credible. When you are living to please man, your "faith" will not work regardless of how many confessions you make.

As far as the power of the tongue is concerned, it is life and death; and my authority, it is Who I Am in Christ. However, it is my conviction that we are not to have faith in our faith. We are to have faith in Almighty God. It is the faith of our Lord Jesus Christ.

When you boil it all down, the question is, *"What must I do?"* Jesus said to just believe on Him as a child. Signs, wonders, miracles, healings, confessions, all of what is in the Word is important, but these are the results of God being your secret place.

"But thou, when thou prayest, enter into thy closet, and when thou hast shut thy door, pray to thy Father which is in secret; and thy Father which seeth in secret shall reward thee openly" (Matthew 6:6). The word *"closet"* in this passage is the Greek word, *"tameion,"* meaning a secret chamber, a chamber used for storage or privacy. It is in the private chamber, that we share intimately all that is in our hearts with the Father, for our treasure is there, and He shares His heart with us.

Matthew 6:6 also speaks of reward. Who is going to reward you? When you are confessing the Word, supplicating, worshipping and thanking God in the secret place, you should rejoice because He will reward you openly.

God's Ultimate Concern

There is also grace for this time, the grace for getting it right. In 1 Corinthians, chapter 11, it says that if we will judge ourselves, we will not be judged by the world. If we do not judge ourselves, then God is going to judge us so that we won't spend eternity in hell. Paul wrote to the Corinthians to deal with the man committing incest in this manner. *"To deliver such an one unto Satan for the destruction of the flesh, that the spirit may be saved in the day of the Lord Jesus"* (1 Corinthians 5:5). God is concerned with the health of our bodies, but He is in greater priority more concerned with our spirits and souls. He wants our bodies healed, but His ultimate concern is where you are going to spend that soul and spirit life in eternity.

Solomon understood the heart of the matter with these last words of Ecclesiastes 12:14, *"For God shall bring every work into judgment, with every secret thing, whether it be good, or whether it be evil."* He was a man of wisdom, and if anybody learned what wild women would do to you, Solomon did. He married the wrong women, ones who did not serve God Almighty, but rather worshipped idols.

Another example is Elijah. Here is a man who challenged hundreds of prophets of Baal, called down fire from heaven, outran a chariot of Ahab in mud, and said, *"If God be God, then serve Him. Why halt ye between two opinions?"* Yet along comes a woman named Jezebel with threats, and it caused him to take off in cowardly fear.

God winked at our child-like foolishness in times past, but He is not going to wink anymore. He is demanding that we grow up and take personal responsibility for our actions. *"And the times of this ignorance God winked at; but now commandeth all men everywhere to repent"* (Acts 17:30).

In Joshua, chapter 7, the story of Achan points to the effect of secret deeds. The Israelites went to battle and were solidly beaten because there was sin in the camp. It was not turned around until obedience to God took place and the sin was purged. Likewise, you are not going to win the battle as a body, when there is sin in your camp. You are not going to win the battle in your home, business, bank account, or personal life, if there is sin in that place.

Joshua complained before God saying things like, *"We don't understand this. You've turned your back on us. You have forsaken us."* God made him to realize that their own sin had done it. Not everybody, but one man's sin stopped the victory of the battle. In like manner, one person's secret sin in a church will affect the entire body.

"Keep back thy servant also from presumptuous sins; let them not have dominion over me: then shall I be upright, and I shall be innocent from the great transgression"(Psalm 19:13). This tells us that God has provided for us the way of escape. Who can know the secret of his own heart and his own life? Only Almighty God can know.

Our secret place must be cleansed by God as we personally go before Him. If we want the life that is sweet, and truth to guide our steps, our thinking must be pure and holy. We need to pray, *"Lord cleanse me from secret sins and hidden faults."*

Let me also warn you that there will be confrontation because of that prayer. You will suddenly dislike the things you are doing and may begin to see yourself as undone. It is because God has heard your cry and will give you grace for your weakness. When that begins to happen, you will also begin to turn away from the trap of the enemy. God will come to your rescue and put in you His ability, strength, power, grace, and boldness.

God had a purpose for straightening out our secret place, and it is not to beat us over the head, or just for the sake of exposing us. As a matter of fact, quite on the contrary, He totally respects the privacy of that place. God is not just telling us the negative side of the secret place. He is also letting us know that if He is that secret place, He will give the reward, and the reward will be public.

Overcoming in the Secret Place

In Revelation 12, God has spoken about overcoming the devil. It is time to put off the weights of self-pity, of self-seeking, and self-grandiosement. We overcome in a three-fold formula. First, we overcome by the blood of the Lamb, Jesus Christ. Second, we overcome by the word of not just any old thing, but by the Word of our testimony. Third, we overcome by being at a place that self does not really matter and that we love our lives not unto death.

Pride may try to rise up, but we cannot allow it. Command its destruction as it concerns you and do not give in to it. Pride is unbelief, doubt, holding on to something that needs to be released. The fellowship of His sufferings, is coming into the revelation that we are no longer emotionally dependent on other people, but we are growing into the fullness of the measure of the stature of the Lord Jesus Christ, without being battered by every doctrine that is blowing around.

Our feet will be planted on the solid rock, the Lord Jesus Christ. He ultimately died for two things, our freedom from sin and disease. We do not have to sin, and if we should slip up, He made provision to make things right again. He bore on His back the stripes for our healing, that is, all that is necessary for our peace, well-being, and prosperity in every area of our lives.

The second part of Daniel 11:32 says, *"...but the people that do know their God shall be strong, and do exploits."* It does not say know their pastor, local prophet, head intercessor, leading evangelist, or any other being but God. To know someone, you must have regular fellowship with that person. You can only know someone's voice if you have heard it frequently.

We have had the advantage of knowing about Jesus through all the wonderful television, videos, tapes, pulpit testimonies, books, and even friends. Yet just knowing about Him, no matter how great the speaker makes Him sound, is not good enough. Knowing about Him will not get you to heaven even if you can quote the entire Bible from memory. To know someone is to be a friend to them, spend time with them, communicate in meaningful exchanges. This is what He wants to be to you. He wants an exchange based on love.

Jesus is Our First Love

We are looking to be the glorious church in this age, but let us examine what happened to just such a church of the past, the church at Ephesus. In the book of Revelation, the Lord is speaking about the seven churches, what was good about them and what needed correction in order for the Spirit to remain there.

To the Ephesian church He declared, *"Nevertheless I have somewhat against thee, because thou hast left thy first love"* (Revelation 2:4). They were no longer excited about Jesus. He was no longer first place in their lives. It is just like a couple who have fallen in love.

Before marrying her, the young man does everything in his ability to please his lady. He carefully grooms himself to look just right, clean crisp shirt, shiny shoes, pressed pants, smelling great.

To her, Prince Charming has nothing over him. She thinks nothing of spending hours primping, getting her hair done to perfection, nails manicured, bubble baths, mud packs, and a whole assortment of other torturous rituals of cosmetic applications. She wears her absolute finest clothes with just the right accessories.

They both think that the other is just about the best thing in the world since sliced bread. They can't wait to be with each other, so the phone is burning up with use during their hours apart. Their dreams and hopes are filled with thoughts of each other and the joy he or she brings.

Then they get married, and after a while, he shows up at the breakfast table with an old stained T-shirt. His face is covered with grubby stubble. His hair is every which way, and to top it off, he has halitosis.

Not much better, she is there scuffling around in a pair of worn out slippers, wearing a dowdy old housecoat that looks like the first one ever made. Her hair has curlers hanging everywhere, surrounding a pasty face in a permanent squint.

After a series of grunts behind a newspaper, they finish breakfast to prepare for their separate lives. He gets himself all cleaned up, looking good, but all he remembers is that frump across the breakfast table. She goes off to watch "As the Stomach Turns" with only the memory of a stubble faced grunter behind a newspaper.

It's no wonder that the file clerk, who looks like she just walked out of a fashion magazine, becomes such a temptation. It's no wonder that Doctor Handsome-Shoes on the latest daytime soap sparks fantasies. This pathetic couple has lost the glamour, the communication, the beauty, and the glory of that first love. When that spark is gone, there is only the form of a relationship left, but there is no power or life in it.

The Lord Our Righteousness

God is jealous for us to have time with Him and show Him that He is our first love. We do that by taking time to pray, read His Word, wait upon Him, praise and worship Him alone. When you do that, there is nothing that He will not move on your behalf. His righteousness becomes our righteousness and it goes before us as we move through this earth.

The Spirit of the Lord is reminding this generation that there is no shadow of turning about God. As He did for others in times past, He desires to do for us. God does not change; He is absolute. *"Jesus Christ the same yesterday, and to day, and for ever"* (Hebrews 13:8).

In some places in Africa, the sun is still used to tell time. They draw a circle on the ground and put a stick in the center. You can watch the shadow of the stick move as time passes, but at noon, the brightest part of the day, there is no shadow. In like manner, there is no shadow of turning with God. He is perfection and there is no variableness in Him.

Because He is Jehovah-Tsidkenu, God my righteousness, He has set me on high and I no longer am sin conscious. Proverbs 4:18 says, *"But the paths of the righteous is like the light of dawn, which shines brighter and brighter until full day"* (Revised Standard Version). As the body of Christ, we are going to grow in our path because He is Jehovah-Tsidkenu, our righteousness, and our path will grow brighter until we come to that place where He is our first love, and we are His glorious church. Then there will be no variableness in us as well.

Allow the Holy Spirit to seal that which He has done throughout these chapters with the following prophecy that came forth during the teaching of the Secret Place, so that the work of God in our lives will be an invincible and irreversible work in our lives.

"Some of you have been delivered from your secret places that were places of sin, abuse, torment, and torture. As Peter was delivered from the prison, so you have been delivered by the Word and the anointing destroying the yokes of bondage. You will walk in a measure of freedom in those areas that have bound you in secret and in fear of man, that they would find out. You are delivered, and the temptation will not be able to tempt you into the enemy's secret trap, for you are delivered from hidden traps.

By My Word and My anointing, I have delivered you, and by the prayers of My people about you. I have not only delivered you, but I have given you strength, and you will be able to stand and not yield to the temptations that you have yielded to before. You shall have eyes that shall be able to see that which you need to see. You will be able to discern when it is a hidden trap.

It has happened as suddenly as it happened on the day of Pentecost when they saw the tongues of fire and they heard the sound of a rushing, mighty wind. So is the work of my Spirit, when He goes deep within you, He comes suddenly, and He lifts suddenly, and the work has been done within you."

Make God your secret place today. Let God, who changes us from faith to faith, and from glory to glory, transform you into the image of the Lord Jesus Christ. To God be the glory!